Body ◇ Mind & Soul   Pelman Institute

I0118809

BMS

Body • Mind & Soul – personal development

Part I

Published by The Pelman Institute

BMS – Body • Mind & Soul – Part I –

BMS is based on the lessons of pelmanism. Pelmanism is developed by the Pelman Institute in 1898 in London. Pelmanism is a very successful philosophy and way of life. Moreover 450.000 people attended the lessons of pelmanism all over the world during the last century. BMS is developed by the Pelman Institute again in 2013; 115 years in between. BMS is a revised version of the primary original Pelmanism lessons.

Author: Paul Heinerman
Editing, design and layout by: Paul Heinerman
Cover by: Paul Heinerman

ISBN: 978-94-90934-00-2   BMS / Body • Mind & Soul
BMS / Body • Mind & Soul - Part I - personal development -
NUR-code: 100 – Educational books general
NUR-code: 248 – Human and society (> 12 years)

For all your questions and remarks: info@pelman.nl

© 2013, Pelman Institute
Pelman Institute, Markkant 31, 4906 KB Oosterhout

"A thoroughly trained and efficient mind is the ONLY universal asset in the world.

In the last issue, everything depends on the strength and quality of your Feelings".

Pelman Institute   BMS

Body • Mind & Soul - personal development

Content   4

Foreword   12

Part I

CHAPTER 1:   A Good Beginning Means a Good Ending   16

CHAPTER 2: Success is First Inside You – Not Outside   28

CHAPTER 3: Study the Signs of the Times   44

CHAPTER 6   Mental Exercises

CHAPTER 7: Health Culture Exercises   88

Part II

"What is your aim in life?"

Body • Mind & Soul - personal development

Part II

Content   8
Foreword   106

Part I

"Believe in Your Star!"

Foreword

In entering upon a new adventure of any kind we must see to it that our minds are attuned to it. For the right understanding of BMS we should realize its purpose and be prepared to follow its method.

Most people know, but some do not, the difference between a science and an art.

A science is organized knowledge. In this sense anatomy is a science, but you may be a master of anatomy while you remain anatomically undeveloped.

So psychology is a science, but you may study psychology to any extent and it will never make a BMS-specialist of you.

For BMS is the art of living and this art is based on psychological principles, just as a course of gymnastic training is based on anatomy. BMS principles include not only theory, but also practice and the prescribed exercises are an essential feature of its discipline.

Realize that every distinctive achievement like a fine poem, a beautiful picture, a prosperous business, or a remunerative invention, had its first origin in the *mind*.

Develop the mind and the higher results are assured. To aim at mental efficiency is not a selfish thing.

You owe it to yourself, to your family and to the world. The better you are, the more you can do for others.

-       *"A thoroughly trained & efficient mind*
        is the only universal asset in the world".

Even money cannot compete with it and is powerless without it. Every country, every trade, every profession is eager to welcome and employ it. It is the open sesame to the best society; it is the key to every kind of.

Finally, we wish to impress this thought on your mind that:

-       *"in the last issue, everything depends on*
        the strength and quality of your Feelings".

A beautiful car, with a wonderful engine, is not service-able without petrol (gas) and ignition. It stands still.

Hence, if you would get the best out of yourself, kindle afresh the fire of enthusiasm and keep it burning.

Follow the instructions and you will get the same benefit that thousands of others have already received and ac-knowledged. Having begun, resolve to go through to the very end. If your time is limited,

BMS a little every day, in order to keep up the continuity.

CHAPTER 1:   A Good Beginning Means a Good Ending

CHAPTER 1   A Good Beginning Means a Good Ending

Our Training:

-       *"our ordinary training is a training in knowledge: what the world needs is a training in power."*

Matthews' Principles of Intellectual Education.

The wealth of educational values contained in BMS is so impressive in quality and so comprehensive in extent, that the expositor of its principles is occasionally embarrassed by the riches of his subject.

He is compelled to seek new ways of telling the world about the larger life which this true science of success offers to everyone.

As each new way must have a beginning, the immediate problem is to discover the best method of introducing BMS to the student who has just enrolled.

What form of literary expression will convey, better than any other, the merits of a system which already enjoys the benefits of 115 years' experience, but which has moved in step with the advance of modern times?

Simplicity, more especially at the outset, should surely be the key-note.

This will most effectively put the reader into possession of the BMS attitude towards life, which is:

-　　*"vital, optimistic, victorious"*.

He will realize that this book about personal development and mental training which he has in his hands right now is not only an efficient instrument, with endorsements from some of the most prominent people in the world, but also a distinctive contribution to the welfare of the society.

It was not for nothing that out of the primary course of BMS, "Pelmanism", the word Pelmanism found its way into the edition of the Oxford Dictionary.

There is just one further detail.

Having decided upon our own approach to the subject, we would now ask you to be equally particular about yours. We will do our best to ensure a clear transmission, but that will not fully meet the case, unless the receiving end is also working well.

Please tune in carefully and adjust the volume to the circumstances: for it is essential that we shall not be troubled by "crackle" and atmospherics.

In other words, make sure that the conditions at your end are as favorable as possible.

No doubt you have ensured immunity from interruption.

Then give us that attention and interest which will assist you so strongly in a clear understanding of what we are about to offer you and if you feel inclined to jot down notes from time to time, well, all the better!

1.1   Your Mental Magnet

We ask you to consider carefully with us now a few facts whose vital importance should not be observed by their evident simplicity.

First, then:

-      *"Something Good is Coming your Way, IF...*

      "Yes?" You say. "If what?"

      If your Mental Magnet is in working order".

For you have such a magnet, although possibly you are not aware of the fact. Good things are coming in your direction all the time, but unless you have the power to *attract* them, they will pass you by.

It is absurd to run away with the idea that good things never come anywhere near you or the place in which you live. They *do*.

The trouble is that you are either ignorant of your possession of a magnet, or it needs re-magnetizing.

Let us look at these alternatives closely.

How does a handsome woman attract attention to herself? Not by saying: "please notice the beauty of my eyes and the perfect symmetry of my features?"

She gets attention without effort, simply because beauty is compelling. It is a magnet.

Now what is your *magnet*? To get at the answer, ask this question:

-       *"what do you desire to have more*
        than anything else in the world?"

For unless you have some such desire, whether vague or crystal-clear, you would hardly have had the incentive to enroll yourself as a BMS-specialist.

Money? Yes, a large percentage of people would say: "money". Fame? Publicity?

No doubt these are very prevalent ambitions. Others would say: "health first". "Prosperity" would have a good representation. Some people would be hesitant, saying: "I don't exactly know".

1.2   Like Attracts Like

We do not propose to draw up a scale of values as to which desires are better than others, for, though with obvious qualifications, this is largely a question of individual circumstances.

The point we want to drive home is this: the folk who do not know what they want, or have no inner harmony and are destitute of strong desires, are without a magnet.

Good things pass them by. There is no attraction.

The man who is keen on making money sets up a magnet in himself and money begins to come his way:

1)   If he has the big-money brain, he gets big money
2)   If he has the medium-money brain, he gets returns accordingly
3)   If he has the small-money brain, he has to be satisfied with results on a lower scale

But it is astonishing how much an average man can pick up if he has a good magnet.

But you see how this principle works out. A man who hates money, or believes the country is going to the dogs, or who tries to make a profit in a line which he utterly detests, is setting up a repulsion, not an attraction.

Good things avoid him.

Chances give him the go-by.

Opportunities fly away at the sight of him.

"Then how does one get such a magnet?" You ask.

"Is it a gift, like feminine beauty?"

"Or can it be developed?"

It is partly a gift and partly the result of sincere training and experience.

The first question, then, is as to what sort of a magnet you have:

1)   How strong are your desires?
2)   How well formulated are your purposes and plans?
3)   Is your engine in good working order?
4)   Are you equipped?

Tonight, or tomorrow, or soon, answer those questions.

They are *your* questions and nobody else can answer them for you. Answering these questions is necessary for you to set your focus at the direction of your life-goal and is achieving your life-goal not the aim we talk about here?

1.2.0   The 7 aspects of Like attracts Alike

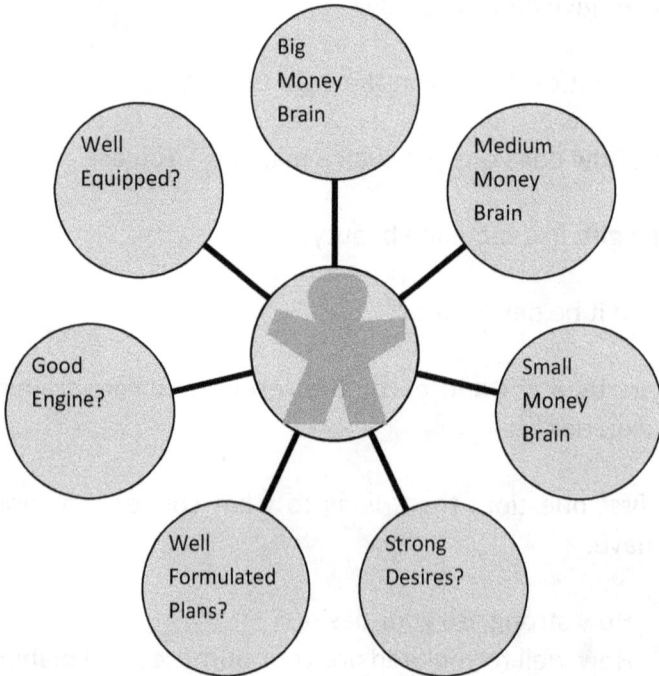

Big Money Brain

Well Equipped?

Medium Money Brain

Good Engine?

Small Money Brain

Well Formulated Plans?

Strong Desires?

Explanation:

As we can see above the first analysis we have to make is the analysis of the state of our brain. Do we possess a big money, medium or small money brain? After that it's also of great importance to know or you have strong desires, also well formulated plans, a good engine and or you are well equipped?

1.3   Opportunity is Looking for Ability

How do we *know* that something good is coming your way?

That is the question, is it not, that you are silently asking us? Here is the answer:

-       *"we know it from observation and experiment"*.

And it is confirmed by leaders of thought and also by the wisdom of the past.

Goethe stated the truth by saying:

-       *"wherefore ever ramble on?*
        For the good is lying near".

The Scottish proverb came nearer the fact by briskly asserting:

-       *"flee you never so fast, your*
        fortune will be at your tail".

It is true that the good, using the word good to embody everything desirable, must be sought after and worked for.

But it is just as true that something good is seeking you.

Emerson, in *Sandi*, urges:

-    *"seek nothing, Fortune seeketh thee."*

-    *"ability is looking for opportunity, but opportunity is also looking for ability"*.

In this first book we are confining our attention to the something good which is coming your way.

And we have just first to convince you that there is this movement in your direction.

At present you doubt it.

You say that you are unable to see it coming.

Quite right: you *are* unable to see it.

And why?

Because your magnet is *"not working"*.

Without equipment you cannot see the something good, any more than a man without a radio set can snatch music out of the air.

So prepare for the good coming to your direction and even much better, expect it and see what will happen.

1.4   The 7 aspects of Something Good is Coming Your Way if

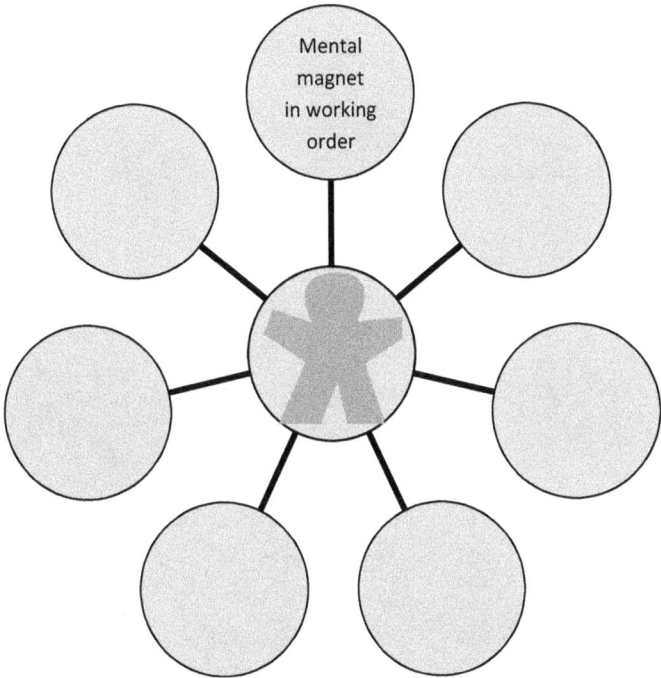

Mental magnet in working order

Explanation:

In this chapter 1 we talked about the first of the 7 Something Goods is Coming Your Way. Of course it is very important for us all to have our mental magnet in good working order.

CHAPTER 2   Success is First Inside You - Not Outside

2.1   Claim What is Yours
2.2   Excellence is Always Victorious
2.3   Thought-Control Means Excellence
2.4   Focused Attention Wins
2.5   What's Coming?
2.6   The 7 aspects of Something Good is Coming Your Way

CHAPTER 2:   Success is First Inside You - Not Outside

But let us take an illustration. Here is a man of 31 who started in business for himself ten years ago.

You might know his name if we mentioned it. He has now a strong following and is doing well. Why? Because, for one thing, he had a good magnet in the form of an attractive personality. People liked to talk to him and he made marketing a pleasure.

Dealers were partial to him because, as they put it, he "had a way with him". A cheerful atmosphere surrounded him and he exuded goodwill.

In consequence, he gathered round him the best people; they went to him for the simple reason that he *drew* them.

All success is first a success *within*.

That is the *"raison d'etre of BMS"*:

1)   It creates in you those qualities which enable you to see the coming good, and to avail yourself of it
2)   It removes all obstacles that stand in your way

In you and we include everybody, in you are powers which at present cannot function.

Self-consciousness and fear, ably supported, it may be, by a wandering mind and a weak will, have so cluttered up your intelligence that you never see the financial and social possibilities which come so close to you that they almost brush you as they pass.

Hence, you do not believe in their existence.

2.1   Claim What is Yours

Turn right-about-face and begin to live for a new and better destiny.

That contest in which you are engaged and which might be called:

-    *"Myself* versus *the World"*,

is one wherein you can be victorious *if* you strengthen all the positive qualities of your nature.

Develop inward power and you will no longer have to seek the good things of life with a despairing heart.

Remember, too, that a certain number of those things are yours by right.

How did Emerson phrase it in one of his more passionate moments?

He wrote:

> *"Has not thy share? On winged feet*
> *Lo! it rushes thee to meet,*
> *And all that Nature made thy own,*
> *Floating in air or pent in stone,*
> *Will rive the hills and swim the sea,*
> *And, like thy shadow, follow thee".*

Will your "something Good" ever catch you up in your life? That depends.

Develop the right conditions and the thing which is yours by right will become yours by actual possession.

2.2 Excellence is Always Victorious

- *"Something Good is Coming your Way, IF...*

    If you Aim at Excellence".

Do you doubt that? Think again.

Why are the leaders of men in those positions of prominence where you see them today?

The statesmen, the bankers, the artists, the manufacturers, the merchants, the novelists and all the rest of them?

Because they know one thing supremely well. Let that sink in. They aimed at excellence and won it.

Consequently, excellent things are coming their way:

-        *"like attracts alike"*.

Money, for instance, makes money because it is sociably inclined.

Money likes company and gravitates where it is found in larger aggregations. You must have noticed that yourself.

The other day a man, journeying North, had to stop because his car refused to move. It was of foreign manufacture and presented unfamiliar internal mechanisms to the three mechanics who one after another tried to make it go. Suddenly a man in overalls came on the scene and the three hailed him.

It was Ned Bailey, the crack motor mechanic of the district. Ned peered inside a minute, adjusted something or other and the car started.

It looked like a miracle. Could Mr. Bailey overhaul the car? The owner asked. No, he couldn't. Was full up for a whole month, all day. And off he went to his next job.

Excellence pays fine dividends.

Did you ever ask yourself why the name Royce meant so much in the motor-car world?

If not, we will ask and answer for you. It meant much because Royce sought *perfection*. Read his life for an inspiration. Mastery!

Did you ever see Pachmann at the piano and listen to his dulcet tones as he interpreted some masterpiece of Chopin?

Have you ever heard Kreisler and marveled when he made the violin speak?

Did it not make you feel that you would like to do your job with the same perfect technique?

"There is something inspiring about excellence in action".

We recall a meeting in which a group of men were trying to settle a complicated highway problem. Half-way through the meeting a new man came in and listened quietly.

He was later appealed to for an opinion of the proposal before the meeting and instantly answered: "it's not the way." In a few minutes' speech he had solved the whole difficulty and with such simplicity that he made the crowd of them look like some amateurs.

Are you *master of anything?*

Book-keeping? The law of contracts? Philosophy, the grocery business, railroading, gardening, radio, the Spanish language, house-building, poetry, art criticism, farming, tailoring, salesmanship?

The thing itself does not matter.

It is the excellence of your knowledge and skill that is important.

A tip-top man in any job is seldom in need of work. Work goes out to find him.

2.3   Thought-Control Means Excellence

But this excellence must appear in our thoughts as well as in our actions. For that matter:

-       *"unless there is first excellence in thought,*
        there will never be excellence in action".

For, as we just pointed out in our Foreword, all distinctive achievements have their first origin in the mind.

Yes, you may perhaps murmur, that stands to reason. I should never plan anything ahead unless I thought about it first.

But many of my thoughts are nothing about success, or excellence, or anything of that sort at all.

I may be wondering whether my train will be late, or which team won the soccer game, or recalling the row I had with that fellow X.

Exactly.

You may well think of all these things and we see no reason at all why you should not.

But you should keep your ideas under your own control and rein them back pretty sharply if they show signs of taking a turn which you had not intended.

If the idea of your train being late suggests an extra ten minutes in bed which you know is not really justified, it is time to change the subject.

Similarly, if an unwise "plunge" results from considering the soccer game, or anger results from recalling Mr. X.

This point will be followed a little further in a later lesson dealing with the subconscious life:

-      *"in the meantime, resolve that you will aim at excellence in thought as well as in deed during the whole day"*.

2.4   Focused Attention Wins

Once again:

-     *"Something Good is Coming your Way, IF...*

    If you have Acquired the Power of Concentration".

Yes, already you know the importance of this power and all that remains for us to do is to drive it home:

-     *"what really tells in life is the*
    whole mind working together".

If you can concentrate, you can put into action every faculty you possess: your perceptions, your memory, your imagination, your power of will.

When Mrs. Mallory had defeated Suzanne Lenglen at Forest Hill, Long Island, women's tennis, she said by way of explanation:

-     *"I set my mind and heart on winning. I did not even know what Suzanne was wearing until the game was over".*

There was concentration personified. Victory came to the Swedish-American woman mainly because she knew how to focus her attention.

And victory will come your way, too, when you have acquired the same power:

1)   What can you expect to do with a mind which flits hither and thither like a butterfly?
2)   How can you hope to get the idea for a much-desired invention?
3)   Can you reasonably look for any betterment in your life until you can sit down and examine facts analytically and get at their true inwardness?

You cannot. But BMS has changed a lot of lives by imparting this secret of concentration.

Is it not a secret worth having?

-      *"Something Good is Coming your Way, IF...*

       If you Organize and Use your Leisure Time".

There are 8.760 hours in a year. Have you ever analyzed the way in which you spend your 8.760?

So many for *sleep,* the number you give to *work,* to *journeying* here and there, to *recreation* and to *leisure.*

So find your laptop or pen and notebook and *"get busy"* on this bit of arithmetic. The result will probably be an eye-opener.

Perhaps the most astonishing item will be the amount of leisure time at your disposal.

Equally astonishing may be the sudden realization of the way in which you are spending it. It is poor economy to be thrifty with one's money and prodigal of one's time.

You feel, perhaps, that you could do much more if you had proper counsel and guidance.

Well, this is what BMS is for:

1) it organizes the mind and all its activities
2) *If time is money* and in one sense it is, then BMS puts money into your pocket, because by showing you how to value your time it prevents you from wasting it
3) You can turn the passing hours to good account now, not only in a commercial but also in a cultural sense. But that is not all. You thereby prepare yourself for that something good which is coming your way
4) It comes because of a fitness which wisely uses your leisure imparts

Without that fitness the good passes you by. You are not ready.

The qualifications are absent.

Thus the choice lies between:

- *"time wisely spent and time spent otherwise?"*

We are not going to point a moral. You can do that for yourself.

All we will do is to remind you of some words from our well known Shakespeare, who, as might be expected, has something to say on this subject:

"Time's the King of men, He's both their parent and he is their grave
and gives them what he will, not what they crave".

Time has not yet been dethroned.

2.5   What's Coming?

Much more is coming:

- *"Something Good is Coming your Way, IF...*

    If you can Read the Signs of the Times".

You know where that sentence comes from.

It is not a financier's phrase, or a banker's, or an economist's, or a market tipster's.

It is a phrase from the greatest of spiritual prophets and he referred to spiritual, imminent changes.

But it is applicable to all sorts of changes.

There are *three questions* which an alert man or woman can profitably ask and answer in regard to his or her own calling:

1) What is happening now?
2) What is going to happen?
3) How can I be ready?

Generally speaking, you know the answer to question 1).

It is question 2) which is more difficult.

When you have answered it, question 3) is made easier.

What changes are coming in your profession or line of business?

And how can you prepare yourself to meet them?

A new development may be on the surface, or it may be deeper down.

It is a surface change when a new style of advertising becomes fashionable for a few years.

It would be a deep-down change if poplar trees took the place of fir as a source of supply for pulp paper, or if rocket propulsion displaced steam, gas and petrol for carrying passengers with speed and safety.

But every kind of change is always in the process of evolution and the benefit goes to the man or woman who sees things before they actually arrive.

2.6   The 7 aspects of Something Good is Coming Your Way if

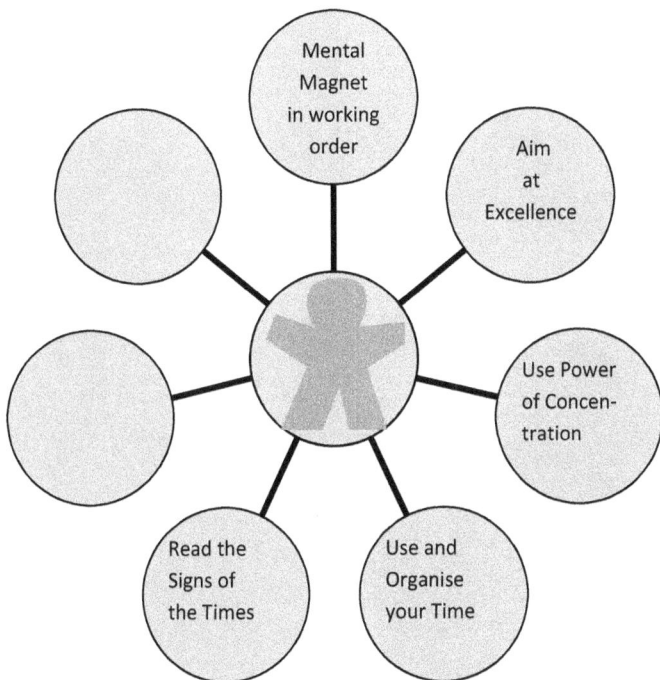

Explanation:

In this chapter 2 we talked about the 2nd, 3rd, 4th and 5th of the 7 Something Goods is Coming Your Way. Aim at Excellence, Use Your Power of Concentration, Use and Organize your (leisure) Time and Read the Signs of the Times.

CHAPTER 3   Study the Signs of the Times

CHAPTER 3   Study the Signs of the Times

New things gravitate to the men who have seen them coming. Did not Alfred Harmsworth see the idea of a new kind of morning newspaper making tracks for his office on Fleet Street? He did.

And why did that idea feel compelled to move in the direction of the man who later became Lord Northcliffe?

Because he studied the signs of the times. He was prepared to offer a welcome. He had a magnet which attracted the something good in his direction.

Your own kind of work will be affected by the progress of the age and if you can divine the coming changes, the adventure will inevitably be yours. Nothing can stop it:

-        *"provided you can make yourself ready for action".*

Events are happening now, the true significance of which we may or may not know.

A long time ago, in a weekly journal, there appeared a picture of a Kentucky village as it was in the year 1809.

Two farmers were talking and the burden of their complaint was that times were dull in the village and nothing ever happened.

"There's just a baby boy born at Tom Lincoln's", said one: "but nothing much ever happens here".

And yet that baby boy when he grew to be a man became great and there is a statute erected to his memory in front of Westminster Abbey. He was Abraham Lincoln.

Now that is the kind of event which we cannot know at the time. But there are others we can know.

Just ahead of us are new developments in many forms of enterprise:

1)   What are they?
2)   When will they become fact?
3)   How will they affect you?
4)   What ought you to do by way of preparation?
5)   Will the coming of space colonization, advanced communications or significant uses of renewable re-sources as alternative energy sources, for example, affect your interests?

Answer these questions and out of the misty future there come benefits that would otherwise have passed you by. And also of a great interest for you is the following.

3.1   Believe in Your Star

Is one of the most important things we will discuss here.

And now, for almost the last time, we repeat:

-       *"Something Good is Coming your Way, IF...*

        If you are a Believer, in yourself".

This is almost our final point in this particular connection and we hope you will consider earnestly whether you are fully convinced of it or whether you have but vague and confused ideas on the subject.

Napoleon once lead a doubter to the window and, pointing through it in broad daylight, demanded: "do you see that star?"

"No", said the man puzzled. "Exactly: I am the only man who can see it", responded Napoleon quietly.

The Something Good *never* gravitates towards the mind that is full of doubt and fears: it moves in the direction of the man or woman who believes.

There is no magnetic force in a brain which believes life is not worth living or that the world in general is rushing to destruction. Such a man has no faith: not even in himself. He repels the good instead of attracting it.

As Falstaff said to the hostess: "there is no more faith in thee than in a stewed prune".

Now what is meant by this *"believing in Yourself?"*

It is, broadly speaking, *self-confidence*. In some people it is instinctive: they accept themselves and the world with satisfaction and proceed to live their life with zest.

They have *natural* faith, sometimes of an intense quality: otherwise we could not explain the presence among us of skeptical men or women who work for the creation of an earthly paradise as the one and only hope of mankind.

Other men or women are intense doubters. They doubt other people and they doubt themselves. If you belong to this class, be assured that BMS will make a vast difference in the quality of your self-feeling, if you will allow it to work.

Doubt will disappear and self-reliance will takes its place!

"The greatest benefit without a doubt to me is Confidence in the future; I have just ceased to doubt myself. BMS has revealed my strongest and best points, which *has made me believe in myself*. Latent personal possibilities have been awakened to an extent which has surprised me. *'I will do it, I'll show them what I can do'*, that is how I feel. Interest, Observation, Right Feeling, Thinking, Acting, it all bring great joy and a lot of profit", said a former student of us.

3.2   Success is for You

Now, let us look back on the ground we have traversed.

When you said, *"If what?"* did you expect something like magic would be imparted to you in the form of a wonderful secret? We ask because so many people think success in life is made by performing miracles. Quite wrong!

Success comes by science and common sense.

And now, for positively the last time, we repeat:

Something Good is Coming Your way if:

-        *"You Believe the Success is for You"*.

That is why our students of BMS are very successful:

1)   It takes the individual and shows him how to get the best out of himself
2)   It does not say: "before you can succeed you must speak five languages and be able to explain Einstein and relativity"
3)   It says: "you, whoever you are, can so prepare your mind that good things will feel the attraction and begin to move in your direction"
4)   BMS tells you: success is first *within* you and "BMS" makes an individual ready to receive

3.3   The 7 aspects of Something Good is Coming Your Way if

Explanation:

In this chapter 3 we talked about the 6th and 7th of the 7 Something Goods is Coming Your Way. Believe in yourself and believe also in your success. Believe in the fact BMS is above all just the setting of a great mind set, yours.

3.4 Some Questions and Answers

Before proceeding to the next section of this book, we ask you to close the book and ponder very carefully over what you have just read.

Do not just accept it passively and still more important, do not dismiss it as holding no direct message for you.

The more thoroughly you turn over in your mind the matters we have discussed, the more numerous will be the points of contact you will detect and the more intimately will they prove to be connected with your own affairs.

And, as an outcome of this careful reflection you will no doubt have developed certain arguments beyond the points to which we have so far taken them.

And, while, if in the course of this extended consideration a doubt or two and a question or two, should have emerged, all the better.

For this will demonstrate that the process of frank co-operation, yours and ours, is already active.

The doubts will be resolved and the questions answered as our principles gradually shape themselves, but in the meantime, we will answer immediately one or two such queries as are frequently put to us.

1.   "How can a misfit job become a true-fit?"

By continuing to be a misfit, as cheerfully as may be, the while he prepares for the true-fit job.

A bookkeeper who hates ledgers and longs to be a salesman can become a salesman if he likes. Of course, if he waits for somebody else to get him ready, he may have to wait a long time.

2.   "Why should we aim at success at all? Why not be content with a moderate efficiency?"

It is essential to aim at something and usually you do not aim at failure, do you? If you sit down to write a letter to someone for whose opinion you care one iota, you try to write not a bad letter but a good one. That is, you aim at success.

When your sports team plays another team, they are all out to win, obviously.

Second-best is of no use to anyone.

3.   "How much drudgery ought a man to put up with?"

Plenty. There is no satisfaction gained in the long run by being niggardly about it. We should show tenacity.

A student reports having seen in Florida some Spanish moss growing on the telegraph wires, not on the posts, but on the wires themselves. That is the type of tenacity we might well emulate. That moss holds tight, and grows by means of air, sun and rain.

Hold on to your job and do well in it, even when the job itself is dull to distraction. There's always a better day coming.

4.   "What reason have I to suppose that BMS will, after all, help in *my* case?"

These principles are based on human nature and developed on lines suggested by 115 years' experience in overcoming the difficulties, both typical and individual and ensuring the success of many thousands of students.

These number of men and women consists of all nationalities, in every conceivable walk of life and covering a very wide range of ages.

In every case they felt the urgent need of guidance, or they would not have bought this book, as you have done. That they just gained such guidance and achieved their purposes is witnessed by their own enthusiastic testimony.

Yet they had also to start at *"scratch"*, as you are doing.

5.   "But what if I am a unique case?"

Everybody is a unique case, to us and in real.

It is precisely the manner in which the essential *unique you* differs from everybody else that constitutes your personality.

We shall help you to develop that personality in full, not to distort or cramp it.

Nevertheless if, in the process, you are assisted to exercise in a more marked degree certain abilities which have so far been thwarted, is that not an enriching of your personality?

Very probably you will prove to be one of those students and their name is legion, who possess certain terrific potentialities that have hitherto lain unsuspected.

These will be freed from their bonds and allowed to operate actively as your full and unique self-realization is achieved.

6.   "Then how can one specific book develop my unique personality?"

Because in the last resort the basic principles of human nature are the same.

CHAPTER 4: Increased Ability – Increased Assets

CHAPTER 4:   Increased Ability – Increased Assets

This is the end of this preliminary section of the first part of this book, but it is only the beginning of the subject for you. Read it again and again until the ideas are part and parcel of your mind itself. Realize the fundamental conception:

-    *"that the best way to succeed in life is not to go here and there seeking for success, but just so to develop your powers that success "comes".*

If you wish to increase your income, the one thing to do is to *increase your ability*:

-    *"the mistake of scores of men and women is to try for larger emoluments without developing their own capacity".*

These larger emoluments will undoubtedly arrive when a greater knowledge and proficiency have been obtained by *"preparing"* for the advance.

The extra income is a *"something good"* which comes to them as soon as they are ready for it. That is the fact behind all the testimonials which stand to the credit of BMS.

It's all about body, mind and soul.

These students did not put money first. They learned:

-    *"that if they acquired greater ability*
     just to do things, the rest will "come". And it did.

Further: there were benefits in addition to money and an addition to our culture, for instance. Some students have said: *"I never really understood poetry until I have gone through the whole series of BMS-books"*.

BMS, truly carried out, *enriches the individual's whole life*.

4.1   The Place of Memory in Mental Efficiency

Memory, that is to say, the power to remember, comprises three factors:

1)   Impression
2)   Retention
3)   Recollection

And if any one of these three factors is impaired, the memory is in a corresponding degree defective.

You are earnestly requested to pay very close attention to this portion of the first part of this book, since it forms a groundwork upon which much of your future success will be built.

4.2   Impressions

Impressions are of two kinds:

1)   those coming to the mind from outside i.e. external impressions and
2)   those arising within the mind itself by the working of thought and of imagination i.e. internal impressions.

Of course, even an internal impression may have roots in previous external impressions, but that does not concern us here:

-    *"ease of the step of recollection depends more upon the strength and vividness of the first impression as well as also upon its emotional coloring and by the associations it sets up".*

4.3   Internal Impressions

When an idea originates within the mind, it is a real good exercise to trace the train of thought that led up to it.

Ask yourself:

1)   Why did that idea occur to me? And ask yourself the next question:
2)   How did it come?

Do not hurry away from it. Turn it over.

Ask yourself what bearing it has upon the department of life, study, or business, with which it may be concerned.

If it is an idea likely to prove of value, recall it to mind after a brief interval.

Later on in the Course, we shall describe various methods of association by which you will be able, so long as the mind retains its normal vigor, to recall an idea in spite of a considerable lapse of time.

But there are other things which you must learn first and for the present you must treat impressions with the means already at your disposal.

We aim at developing your natural memory, not at giving you an artificial one.

If we provide special aids too early in the Course, you will be tempted to trust too much to them and too little to the customary use of your natural powers.

4.4   External Impressions

Although there is a certain class of impressions which originates within the mind itself, there is another and very large class which comes from outside.

These impressions reach the brain through the senses. Sometimes impressions are conveyed to the brain by two or more senses simultaneously.

Thus, when you meet a stranger who begins at once to talk to you, your brain will receive impressions of his appearance and of his speech and these impressions arrive together.

Individuals varies much in their susceptibility to impressions through the different senses, some receiving their most intense impressions by sight; others by hearing:

- *"if you want a perfect memory, you must train not only your powers of reason and association, but also your senses".*

Take a sheet of paper and try to draw upon it the Roman figures exactly as they appear on the face of a clock and then compare carefully the figure you have placed at *"four o'clock"* with the figure as represented on the dial of a watch or clock. A large percentage of persons will not succeed and to fail is indicative of faulty observation.

On which side are the buttons on a man's coat and on a woman's respectively?

Many such details as these have come constantly before your eyes, but have you really *seen* them?

To train your sense of hearing, just try to recognize your friends by their footsteps when they are within hearing, but out of sight. Notice rapidity, regularity and weight and try also to estimate the distance between you and him.

4.5   Retention

The second stage in the process of memory is Retention.

This, so far as it depends upon the physiological condition of the nervous system, may be beyond the direct control of the student:

-    *"however, we may say that whenever a vivid impression conveying a different meaning and affected somewhat by emotion is made, retention is vastly more probable than when the impression is slight and superficial"*.

Of course, if no impression has been made upon the mind, no impression can be retained.

When people say they have *"forgotten"*, they frequently suppose that their retentive power has broken down.

The failure, however, is usually found to be not in the retentive power, but in the third stage, which is the power of Recollection.

A multitude of small details or occurrences which would ordinarily be described as *"forgotten"*, require only the right stimulus to bring them vividly back into consciousness.

The stimulus need not even be of great intensity; for often the passing fragrance of a flower, as everybody knows, will give us back the picture of the peaceful country of our early days, even though we may never have had a thought of it for months or perhaps years.

4.6   Recollection

Recollection is the name given to the revival of an impression made upon the brain and retained by it.

Frequently the word is used as though it were synonymous with *"memory"*.

But in truth recollection is only the third and final stage of the complete process.

Facility in recollection depends:

1)   primarily upon the intensity of the first impression and
2)   in the second place, it depends upon certain principles of association which will be explained in a later book

Recollection may be brought about in various ways:

1) Sometimes it is stimulated by a recurrence of the conditions which originated the first impression.

    Thus if you *"forgot"* an idea you will often find yourself able to *"remember"* it if you return to the exact spot where the idea first occurred to you.

2) Sometimes a single circumstance will recall a whole group of ideas, as when the name of a novelist brings instantly to your recollection the incidents in various books of which he is the author.

3) Sometimes an idea is recalled when its exact opposite is presented to the mind.

    Various theories have been suggested to account for the way in which ideas recall one another into consciousness.

It is enough here to say that everything happens as though the rise to consciousness of each idea were accompanied by the excitation of some group of nervous elements in the brain.

And as though the nervous current were liable to strike across from one group of nervous elements to another group of nervous elements.

4.7   The 7 steps in the Process of Memory summarized

The Process of Memory in 7 steps:

1)   Impression
2)   Internal impression
3)   External impression
4)   Retention affected by vividness and emotion
5)   Recollection
6)   Affected by the intensity of the first impression
7)   Affected by the principles of association

See the scheme besides. The schemes will help you to memorize the information put forward to you in this book much easier. The visual aspect will help your mind in the process of retention and in the process of recollection.

4.8   Concluding Remarks

This is a *Course* of personal development which extends to seven books and each book in this Course will help you to find your answer: *"your unique calling",* in this world.

Each book will also contribute its own quota to your own unique personal development.

You may not see now at once how the exercises which follow are going to help you, but we can see it and we shall, in later pages, make it plain to you.

4.7.0   The 7 steps in the Process of Memory in a scheme

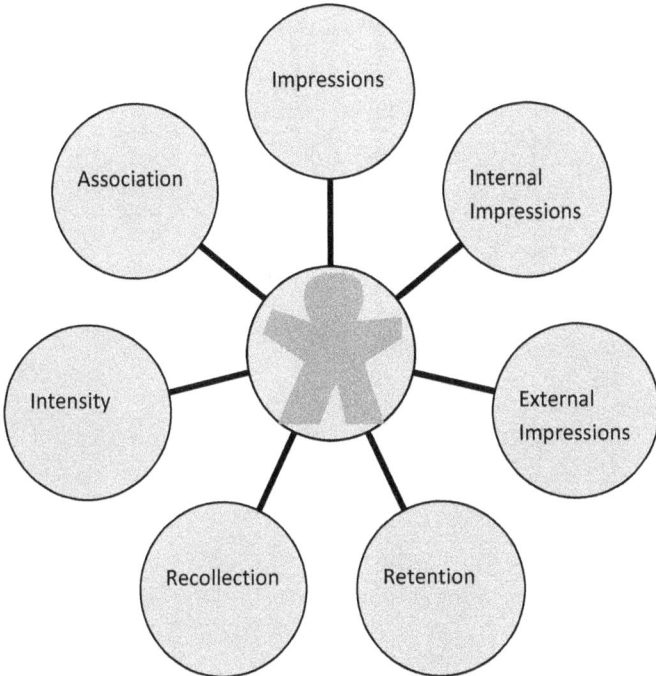

Explanation:

We use schemes as above from a didactic point of view. In the scheme above we can see the process of memory in 7 steps. The schemes will help you to memorize the information put forward to you in this book much easier. The visual aspect will help your mind in the process of retention and in the process of recollection.

CHAPTER 5:   "What to Do – What to Avoid"

5.1   What to Do
5.1.0   The 7 "to Do's" of part I in a scheme
5.2   What to Avoid
5.2.0   The 7 "to Avoid's" of part I in a scheme

5.1   What to Do

"What to Do":

1.   *Work patiently.* There is no magic in BMS, but if you will stick to it the results will be so surprising as to take on the *appearance* of magic.

2.   Begin to *exercise your Will-power now.* Resolve to master this part I in spite of every difficulty.

3.   Mental Training means the *training of the whole mind,* so just begin and start at once to follow out our instructions in this respect.

4.   You may not see immediately how each part of this book can train the whole mind, but you will realize it later. *The mind is a unity,* not a group of completely separate faculties.

5.   *Emphasize the personal element.* Tell yourself that this BMS-method has a message for *you;* also a discipline, an illumination and a deliverance from error.

6.   *"I have a future with promise in it".* Turn that phrase over in your mind. It is true enough for most people at any rate, but we want you to *feel* it. Then you will act accordingly.

7.   *Believe in your success* and you will attract it.

5.1.0   The 7 "to Do's" of Part I in a scheme

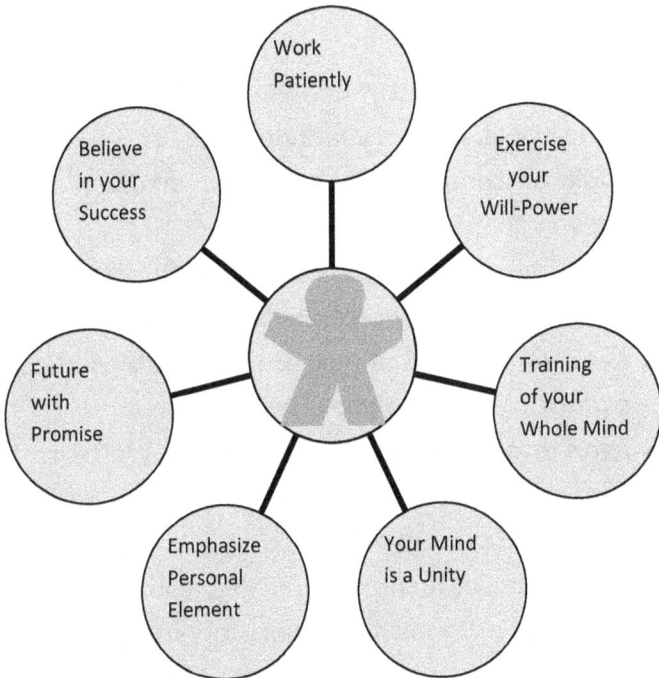

Explanation:

In this chapter 5 we summarized the 7 to Do's of part I of this book. Just try to follow up all the advices we will give you and soon you will experience & see what will happen.

Your real power will grow and grow, your Power to Act.

5.2   What to Avoid

"What to Avoid":

1.   Avoid the idea that your own specific difficulties are insuperable. *Cherish your hopes.*
2.   Avoid all complaining about your memory; that is the way to make it worse.
3.   Avoid the saying: *"I can't concentrate".* It will make you less able to concentrate tomorrow.
4.   Avoid the feeling that you are too old. *Mental age is a matter of training and discipline.*
5.   Avoid haste. Master every sentence. We teach the science and art of mental efficiency in the least possible of printed pages.
6.   And if you have the notion that you can become mentally efficient by means of studying a few pages, just get rid of this notion. There are 7 books and some work ahead of you.
7.   Avoid the idea that real success is *"not for you"* and just for all the others. The success belongs also to you. Believe in it and *feel it* and you will attract it.

Above we see seven examples of a misuse of your *"self-language"*. Please be aware of the fact that the messages you tell yourself will have great impact on your whole life.

5.2.0   The 7 "to Avoid's" of part I in a scheme

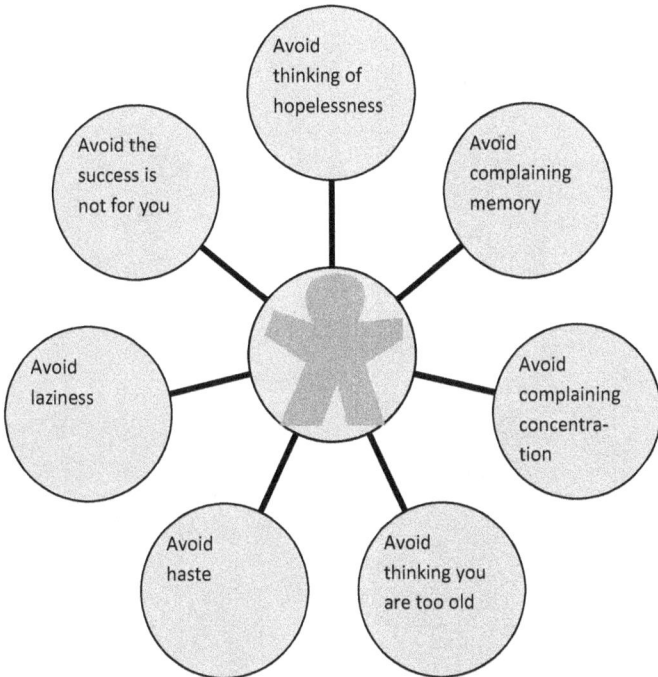

Avoid thinking of hopelessness

Avoid complaining memory

Avoid the success is not for you

Avoid laziness

Avoid complaining concentra-tion

Avoid haste

Avoid thinking you are too old

Explanation:

In this chapter 5 we summarized the 7 "to Avoid's" of part I of this book. Just see we try to bring you in a mood that your spirit will rise up again and will be able to cherish and flourish again. Just try to avoid these demotivating 7. To control your *"self-language"* is part of your success.

CHAPTER 6　　Mental Exercises

CHAPTER 6   Mental Exercises

Now it is time for us to transform our study results in some action and exercises.

6.1   Exercises and Experience

There are 2 methods of developing your personal powers:

1)   by the acquiring of knowledge about mental operations and
2)   by the practice of exercises

Both methods are necessary if you would like to obtain the full benefits of BMS. That is how your mind becomes experienced and experience has been defined as:

-     *"the process of becoming expert by experiment"*.

This also applies to the physical exercises, specially devised by experts for the benefit of BMS students.

You are urged to practice these Exercises because they will help in:

1)   promoting health
2)   producing energy and
3)   because they will directly and indirectly assist in your mental development

6.2   Exercises and the Right Point of View

It is essential at the outset to regard all the prescribed Exercises in the right way.

The wrong way is to think that they do not really matter and that the teaching of the lessons is the one important thing:

-     *"the teaching is important, without any doubt, but practice if anything, is even a little more important"*.

You would not think of taking a course of physical training and confining your attention to reading the instructions and gazing at the illustrations of body movements.

You would practice *daily*:

-     *"Mental Training should be pursued in the same way, continuous and regular practice is needed"*.

For instance, an elderly student pupil writes:

"BMS has brought home to me the fact that just as nearly twenty years ago I had to begin to do a set of physical culture exercises daily in order to preserve my health and keep physically fit, so in order to keep my mind alert and active I must daily practice mental exercises also and those suggested in the Course cannot be surpassed.

"Although I have been familiar with theoretical psychology and its pedagogical application for forty years or so, BMS has brought my knowledge to a personal focus and applied it to my own case in a way I had never dreamt of. It has set up for me a higher ideal of mental and physical culture than ever and has shown me how it can be achieved by steady, constant daily effort". Teacher (aged 57).

We do not wish to over-emphasize this requirement.

What we stress more than anything is the *"immense advantage"* which steady and regular daily practice will be to you personally. That fact alone should make it an ideal that is worthwhile.

There is another point to be remembered. A few of the Exercises appear to be so simple that the student may imagine they will be of little service to him. This is a serious mistake.

In physical culture the movements of the limbs and of the body generally, are simple enough, but they do wonders for health and strength.

Similarly, some of the simpler BMS Exercises are highly effective for mental development.

Please bear this in mind. Naturally some of the Exercises are not so easy. That is to be expected.

6.3   Your Note Book

Purchase a suitable Note Book or use your Laptop in which to record your thoughts and impressions, also any data which are deemed of value:

-       *"incidentally, this note-taking, if carefully carried out, will assist you in acquiring the great art of your unique Self-expression".*

6.4   Mental Exercises

Now it is time to practice some mental exercises in real.

6.4.1   Exercise 1   Sight and Hearing

The first scientific step in mental training is to educate the powers through which most of our information comes, namely: *sight* and *hearing*.

Take a sheet of paper and write down the list of the names of six of your friends, three of each sex.

Opposite each name write:

1)   the color of the eyes
2)   the nature of the complexion
3)   the manner of wearing the hair, the color of the hair and

4)   in the case of the men, the absence or presence of sideburns, beard and eventually a mustache
5)   add also a note as to any special or particular article of clothing worn on the last occasion you saw the person concerned

Some people find an exercise of this kind very easy: they are naturally acute observers. Others find it rather difficult: their powers need training.

It is the object of this exercise to discover the extent to which you observe people and things and to stimulate you to build up a habit of personal observation:

-   *"test yourself occasionally by means of it throughout the Course in order to see how you are yourself developing in observational power"*.

6.4.2   Exercise 2   Sense Appeals

Take up a position inside the home or outside, anywhere, indeed, where sense appeals are possible and after five minutes write down what you have seen, heard, or otherwise experienced. As a Specimen of Report you might write something like this:

"I heard a train whistle and a motor car honked in the distance. Saw a swallow fly past the window. Heard a strange sound several times, but could not identify it.

Smelt frying bacon from next door and wondered on what food the pigs had been fed. Counted the shades of green in the foliage. Distinguished five, wind from south east, heavy clouds coming up; temperature cooler than yesterday".

6.4.3   Exercise 3   Playing Cards

Deal out four playing cards, face downward, side by side. Turn up the first and note what it is, replacing it face downward. Repeat the process with the three other cards; then, after two minutes, try to recall the four in order.

When you can do this correctly, experiment with five cards, taking different cards each time and as you gain in confidence gradually increase the number.

As this is an exercise for the visual imagery we want you to rely as much as you can upon the visual impression.

After a period of this sight training you can amuse yourself and your friends by asking them to place about a dozen articles upon a table: matchboxes, spoons, paperweights, penknives, eyeglasses, anything; each object being slightly separated from the others.

Let them be covered with a cloth or with a small tray while you are out of the room.

No matter how quickly they lift the cover and replace it again, you should be able to name a majority out of a dozen or more articles.

6.4.4   Exercise 4   Ticking of a Watch

It is interesting and useful to know at what distance removed from you the ticking of a watch can be heard.

Deafness is a matter of degree and often even a matter of inattention.

Sometimes minor defects in hearing, quite remediable in their early stages, are allowed to develop unnoticed.

We advise all students who find reason to doubt whether their sight and hearing are normal, to have their eyes and ears tested by qualified practitioners.

Acuteness of hearing can be cultivated and it is worthwhile to increase by inches the distance between you and the watch, so as to determine the ratio of improvement.

Thus, if on a first attempt you can hear a watch ticking on a table five feet off, stand a foot farther away, then another foot and so on, until you fail to hear the sound.

Use the same watch always and in the same place if possible.

These exercises in Perception are not intended to discourage the student by showing him wherein he is deficient:

-     *"all we aim at is to develop efficient sense-power in each case, because such a development means a real intellectual advance".*

6.4.5   Exercise 5   Association

-     *"Whenever there is a connection between two ideas, or between the words representing two ideas, the connection is based on certain relations grouped under the general heading of Association".*

A special book on these relations will be given later on in this series of 7 books and the mastery of it will enable you to write down 1.000 or more words and having read them over once to repeat the whole list from beginning to end, or from the end to the beginning.

At present we shall do no more than illustrate the fact that such a connection does exist.

Here, for instance, is a list of eight words.

By way of exercise read them through once.

Note the way in which the first is related to the second, the second to the third and so on.

Then repeat them, or as many of them as you can:

1)   White
2)   Red
3)   Stars
4)   Stripes
5)   America
6)   Canada
7)   Can
8)   Tin

6.4.6   Exercise 6   Walk in Country and listen to sounds

Take a walk in the country and sit down.

Listen to the sounds you can hear.

From what direction do they come?

How many are there and what is the difference between them?

Afterwards, when reading nature descriptions, compare your knowledge of sounds with that of the author.

If you cannot easily get into the country, adapt the exercise to the sounds of the city.

We advise you to practice this exercise on a daily basis.

6.4.7   Exercise 7   End of day Review

At the end of each day, or as often as you can, review all that has happened, in the order of its happenings, from the moment of waking.

This does not refer to trivial details, although these will occur to you as you pass from one event to another.

We mean the more significant items such as your own conversations in person and eventually some by sms, your phone calls, your meetings, news items, interviews, decisions, resolves, dates for future action and so on.

This is one of the oldest of mental training Exercises and it is one of the best, as you will prove by experience.

From a didactic point of view we have put these seven exercises in a scheme again so you can and will remember the seven different mental exercises more easily.

6.4.8   The 7 Mental Exercises in a scheme

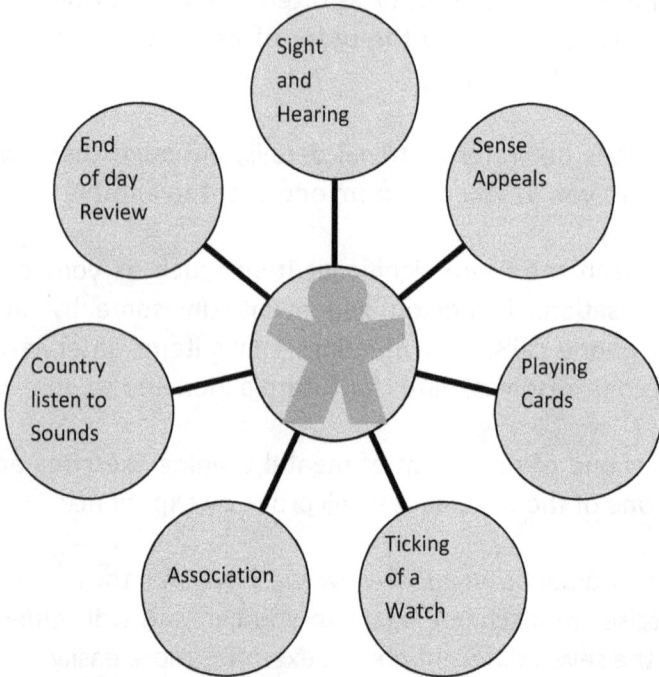

Explanation:

As we can see in the scheme above the mental exercises of Part I give us the opportunity to train our senses, our sight and hear, but also our memory. A thoroughly mental training will give you great results in the near future.

CHAPTER 7:　Health Culture Exercises

CHAPTER 7   Health Culture Exercises

These exercises are especially designed to assist in the development of mental efficiency according to the principles of BMS.

7.1   Introduction

The exercises given in connection with this and the following books are designed to help the student to maintain or improve his physical efficiency.

And also to aid those students who feel that their efficiency needs to be increased.

They are designed to help those students who have been careless about their physical condition or who have become *"run down"* through physical or mental strain.

They are not designed to help the abnormal or as we call it the *"pathological"* sufferer.

In this scheme of efficiency development the main idea is that just a few moments of intensive effort with a corresponding mental concentration will be productive of:

1)   greater benefit than hours spent in a gymnasium doing stock exercises in a casual manner without intensive effort and

2)   without the kind of concentrated self-interest that brings the mental and muscular machinery fully and intelligently into play

The ten minutes spent before the looking-glass on the exercises that follow will give visible and tangible evidence of what body and mind are actually doing.

As a result, the interest of the student is kept at a high pitch, a thing that does not generally happen in circumstances where the effects are vague and invisible, as they usually are in the customary gymnasium exercises.

The exercises are planned on a system extensively used by Gymnasts.

Briefly and technically stated, the order of progression in each individual set of your seven Supplementary Health Culture Lessons, is as follows:

1)   Introductory – Elevators – Getting Up etc.
2)   Corrective – Stretching – Stand Straight etc.
3)   Hygienic – Warming Up – Windmill – Frog Jump etc.
4)   Recreational – Golf Drive – Swimming – Fencing etc.

But while each book follows this general scheme it also has a special purpose. The purpose of emphasizing the use of some particular group of muscles under the direction of some special kind of mental effort.

There is therefore a progressive development of mental and physical power as you go from one book to the next.

This special purpose is indicated at the beginning of each of the seven sets of exercises. Keep this in mind as you work.

The breaking down of your physical efficiency has been gradual.

So be aware of the fact that:

-        *"the process of restoring and increasing
         your own efficiency will also take time".*

There is no idea of *"get strong quick"* or *"get thin quick"* in this course.

The exercises are primarily for the purpose of obtaining the greatest value and efficiency of the highest kind, both in mind and body, for healthful, happy living and for success in all walks of life and to show your uniqueness.

7.2   Warning

Each student must judge his own strength in doing these exercises. If you will guard against overdoing them at first, you will obtain results more quickly.

We advise that you should take each exercise very easily for the first time, more with the idea of getting the position and movements correctly than of exerting any great amount of energy.

As you become accustomed to the movements, gradually increase the energy with which you do them.

7.3   Physical exercises

All animals, when awakened from slumber, stretch first one set of muscles, then another. They do this to stimulate the blood supply and to *"get the kinks out"*. So we too should try to restore a balanced circulation before starting our day.

To jump out of a warm bed and rush into a bath or into one's clothes is wrong.

Eight hours, more or less, of quiet rest had left a sluggish circulation, stiff muscles, or a cramped feeling.

The heart's action has been reduced because nature had taken the precaution to conserve energy during rest.

In order to re-establish the functioning of the body in a healthful manner, one should follow the example of the cat and loll a bit, stretch a bit, yawn a bit and give the muscles the time to prepare for the demands of the day.

7.3.1   Physical exercise 1   Elevator

On getting out of bed, while the bath of lukewarm water is filling, stand before a mirror, feet together and head erect and, while slowly raising the arms from the side to overhead, open your mouth and take in a good supply of fresh air.

Do not *"duck"* or bow your head as you raise your arms.

Keep watching the position of your head and chest in the mirror. With your lungs well filled with air, try to raise your chest toward your chin. Try hard for two seconds but do not strain.

Then slowly lower the arms and chest and exhale.

Repeat this for two or three times, always strongly but without straining.

Try to increase the elevation of your chest.

Rest for ten seconds now, enjoying the tingling sensation which the increased blood supply has brought you.

Suggestion:

Inhale;   raise chest higher, just a little higher and count: *"One, two, three"*, slowly.

Exhale;   while counting: *"One, two, three, four, five"*.
             Repeat.

Purpose:

-      *"to develop the chest and to increase
       the unique capacity of your lungs"*.

7.3.2   Physical Exercise 2   Stand Straight

Purpose:

-      *"a good body position is just the greatest help to a
       normal functioning of the bodily organs so try to
       stand straight"*.

You have a door in your room: stand with your heels,
hips, back and the back of your head, against the edge of
the door.

Study:

-      *"the feel of the straight spine"*.

Notice the decided mental response to the body position
and then make up your mind to assume that position several times during the day. Determine to acquire the
"straight-standing-against-the-door" position permanently. This training is all about replacing bad habits in better.

7.3.3   Physical Exercise 3   Warming Up

Standing away from the door, raise your arms sideways to shoulder level. Now swing the arms loosely and easily across your body until your hands slap against your shoulder blades, or as far back as possible.

Swing the arms backwards and forwards a dozen times, just as a man would do on a bitter cold day to stimulate the circulation in his arms and hands.

Listen to the slapping of your hands against the flesh on your back as it *"wakes up"* the sluggish circulation.

This is called the: *"warming-up exercise"*.

Make your movements rapid and your circles or swings in the greatest arc possible. Repeat four or five times.

7.3.4   Physical Exercise 4   Toe Touch

With the arms at the height of the shoulders and out to the sides, spread your feet apart about 18 inches.

Now swing down slowly with the left hand.

Bending forward and twisting to the right and touch your left hand to the floor behind your right heel on the outside of the foot. Bend the knee if necessary.

Raise the body to the starting position and then repeat the exercise on the left side.

Four times right and four times left is enough to start with.

Watch yourself in the mirror to compare your position with that of the instruction above.

7.3.5   Physical Exercise 5   Incline

With the arms still out at the side, transfer your weight to your left foot.

Raise the right knee waist high with both hands and pull it up to against your abdomen.

If possible, hold it in this position for a second.

Incline is to move yourself to a lower position.

This means that you must learn to balance yourself on one foot. Then stretch the leg downwards and backwards until the toe touches the floor as far back as possible.

As the leg goes back, swing the body forward with the arms and your fingers pointing straight downwards and now just bend your left knee until your fingertips touch the floor.

From this position *"pull yourself together"* until you are again in the position with the knee against the chest.

Repeat four times slowly.

Then do the whole exercise again, but this time with the right foot on the floor. This exercise will get your abdominal muscles ready for you to enjoy your breakfast.

7.3.6   Physical Exercise 6   Hopi Dance

Now, to close our ten minutes of efficiency exercises, we must stimulate a more rapid action of the heart.

For this, we will imitate the Hopi Indian dancers.

Raise the right knee upward toward the chest, bending the body slightly forward from the waist.

At the same time, raise your left arm upward over the head. Lower the leg and arm.

Repeat the same movements, using the left knee and the right arm.

Now alternate the two movements about as rapidly as you would if you were performing them to the time of a march. In order to make it a real Hopi step, raise the left knee and the right arm as before.

In this position take a short hop on the right foot.

Then raise-hop-lower-raise-hop-lower in a kind of march or fox-trot time:

-       *"by inserting a little hop with the foot that
        is on the floor you complete the imitation".*

Repeat for five times on each foot.

7.3.7   Physical Exercise 7   Rubbing Body in bath

Now, just a suggestion about your bath. Use lukewarm water and a pure soap.

Vigorous rubbing of the body, arms and legs, excites the dermal nerve-endings and the skin capillaries to greater activity.

Do not lie or sit in the bath; stand up and keep in motion.

Finish the bath with a cool shower or sponge.

Be very careful to dry the body completely.

Dress quickly and avoid all draughts.

It is poor hygiene to immerse the body for any lengths of time after exercise and before eating.

We also always advise our students to take a cool shower:

-        *"the cool shower or sponge is in reality*
         a splendid preventive of so-called "colds".

If you are not in the habit of exercising, your first expe-rience may result in some slight soreness or stiffness or discomfort the first night following or the next morning.

That is a natural consequence.

Do not allow it to worry you.

The exercises of the next morning will remove again the discomfort.

From a didactic perspective we have put the 7 physical exercises of Part I of this book again in a scheme besides.

Starting your morning with each of the 7 exercises above will bring you a great feeling of joy and happiness. It's great to start your day each time with these exercises so just do yourself a big favor and do the exercises each day.

The Elevator, Stand Straight, Warming Up, Toe Touch, Incline, Hopi Dance and Rubbing your Body in bath; all these exercises will help you by achieving your goals in life as quickly as possible.

7.4   The 7 Mental Exercises in a scheme

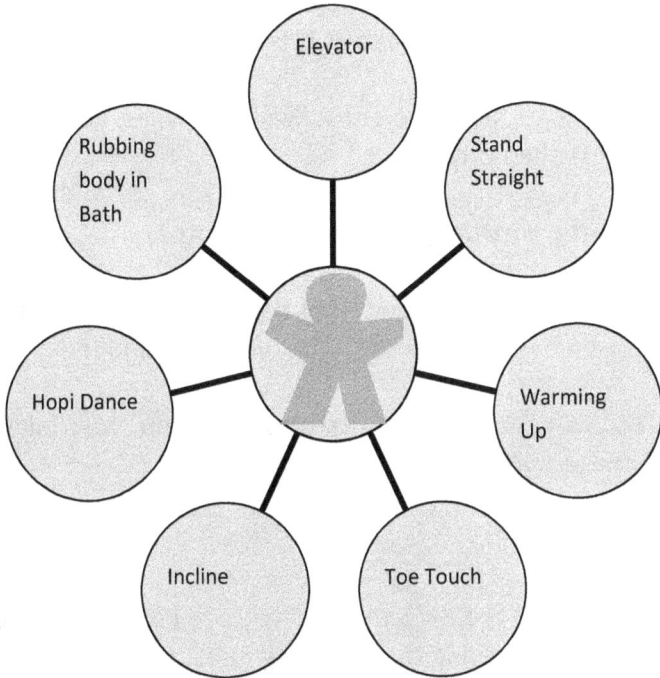

Explanation:

Starting your morning with each of the 7 exercises above will bring you a great feeling of joy and happiness. It's great to start your day each time with these exercises so just do yourself a big favor and do the exercises each day.

7.5 Suggestions for the Day

- *"get some out-of-door exercise each day, try a brisk walk of about 1000 meters".*

Hold the head high, the chest well up, swing your arms well across the body.

And breathe very deeply every few minutes.

Think for instance of your Hopi dance as you step along and just enjoy what you see, what you hear and feel.

Don't take your business troubles with you. Just take a congenial companion.

7.6 Self Coaching

As a student of the BMS-method you are invited to coach yourself by answering the following questions.

7.6.1 Question 1 Your Mental Magnet

What sort of a magnet do you have?

1) How strong are your desires?
2) How well formulated are your purposes and plans?
3) Is your engine in good working order?
4) Are you equipped?

7.6.2   Question 2   Questions in Regard to your Calling

There are three questions which an alert man or woman can profitably ask and answer in regard to his or her own calling:

1)   What is happening now?
2)   What is going to happen?
3)   How can I be ready?

7.6.3   Question 3   Aim in Life

What is your Aim in Life?

7.7   Part II of this book

What is your Aim in Life?

- Have you a definite purpose which you are carrying out with enthusiasm?
- Or, are you drifting, just going where the tide of circumstances takes you?
- Or, are you steering a course for a chosen destiny?

These are real questions demanding real answers.

Part II of this book will help you to find these answers.

Part II

"What is your Aim in Life?"

CHAPTER 1:   Interest

FOREWORD

This is one of the most vital Lessons of the whole Course. It strikes a note that will be heard again.

It asks a question that demands an answer. Some students will be able to answer it off-hand. Many will require time for consideration.

Look at your life as a whole and ask this question:

-        *"what am I aiming at?"*

Have you a ready answer? Have you an answer at all?

If not, you are losing ground all the time.

You are *drifting*. Your growth, both mental and moral, is retarded. We do not mean that you are a failure. Far from it. What we desire to make evident is that if you are devoid of a crystal-clear purpose you are not getting the best out of yourself.

So please study the following part of this book closely.

And study it cheerfully, even if it shows where hitherto you have missed the mark.

Remember that a better day is dawning.

CHAPTER 1:   Interest

Interest is one of the most important subjects to know about if you want to develop yourself fast and complete.

1.1   What do we mean by Interest?

What we mean by interest:

-    *"the soul which has no fixed purpose in life is lost; to be everywhere is to be nowhere"*.   Montaigne.

In order to get the best out of yourself *you must have* an aim in life:

1)   not a general aim, but a particular aim
2)   not a mere desire to be successful in everything that you undertake, but a definite purpose to accomplish a definite end.

There are many reasons for this.

And chief among them is that without a proper plan of life your mental ability will not be developed.

A *wish* is not an *aim*.

As it is highly important that this truth should be realized to the full, we propose to discuss it in greater detail.

1.2   Consciousness of Aim

What does an aim, or purpose imply? It implies that you are moved by a specific desire or *strong feeling* to:

- be an artist
- abolish intemperance
- enter the field of big business
- develop a useful invention
- write a distinctive novel
- make a name for yourself in politics or
- simply and properly make some headway in your present calling and thus obtain an increase in your income

In your mind there must be a clear *idea*, which means that your intellectual powers are intimately concerned with your aim, but the idea is so suffused with emotion that one naturally calls it more a Feeling than a Thought.

There is more *heart* in it than *head*.

The significance of Feeling, as a mental function, becomes evident when it is realized that a strong desire to:

1) achieve
2) attain
3) master
4) conquer

— *"is the basis of every plan of life".*

There are good desires and there are bad ones.

There are others which might be described as neutral.

Consequently, when formulated and acted upon, some are found to be beneficial in results just as others are obviously injurious.

In every case it will be found that *Feeling* is the motive-power that stimulates the intelligence and prompts the will to action.

But the desire that is truly effective is no simple willing-ness to receive, it is more than a mere wish to possess, it is positive, purposeful and energetic.

What then is this Feeling? In a general sense it is just *"Interest"*. Take games as an illustration.

1) Why do you sit for hours watching a football or bas-ketball match? Because you are really interested in the play and wish your side to win.
2) Why do you and others devote two evenings a week to physical drill or to games, to languages or to public affairs? Simply because you and they have an interest in these things. Other men have other interests and act accordingly.

The tragic thing is to have *no* defined interest at all.

It spells mental decay, unhappiness and often disaster.

If you will read the biographies of leaders of thought and men of action, you will find that in every case the motive power was that of Interest.

And it manifested itself in two ways:

1)   an end was in view and
2)   means for attaining that end were devised

They were *ambitious*.

Do not imagine that only Statesmen with world-designs are ambitious, or Oil and Railway magnates, or would-be Members of Parliament.

We are all ambitious, or we should be, so long as our ambitions are just.

The student who has secured his Arts degree passes on to the Doctorate and has his eye on a professorship.

Why not?

1)   He is interested in his work
2)   He has formed a plan of action

3) He contributes to published magazines and trade journals and

4) although he may not care to acknowledge it in so many words, he is just as ambitious as a lawyer or doctor is to increase his own *clientèle* or a business merchant to enlarge his profits

The young poet, whose first book was a success, is eager to do finer work.

The newspaper critic who sometimes has an anonymous fling at self-made men and other persons objectionable to him, is secretly indulging hopes of being an editor, or of owning a newspaper himself some day.

We do not regard money-getting and success as synonymous terms. To us, a kind of success is inherent in the very effort to achieve a great purpose.

Even though it fall short of actual achievement for now.

A great purpose:

- *"by great purposes we mean purposes that are great relative to the mind that conceives them".*

A grocer's assistant who hopes and strives for a big shop of his own in ten years' time, is moved by a great purpose.

Just as surely as an astronomer who is determined to solve the mystery of sun-spots, or a pathologist who wills to discover a cure for cancer.

1.3   The Forward Look

All progressive men and women, whether in the Politics, Business, Army, the Navy, the Church or the Law, feel this inward something urging them forward.

Sometimes it is called *"the emotional drive"*.

They have ideals to aim at, purposes to be fulfilled, ends to be achieved:

1)   In Literature it is the writing of a book
2)   In Commerce it may be the possession of a world-wide business
3)   In other cases, again, it is the more modest aim to secure a competency for old age

A few will look forward to becoming amateur champions in golf or tennis, or some other form of recreation.

This Feeling at the basis of our more significant actions is manifested in an Interest that discovers itself in a plan of campaign or action. Each success, however big or small starts with an Interest. It starts with an interest in something or someone. Interest is the key-word right here.

1.4   Interest and Mental Synthesis

We have now to show how this Interest and Aim help you in the development of *your mental ability*.

At first:

-        *"they give the mind Unity of Action"*.

Let us imagine a case. A young man has just left college and begins to look about for some form of employment.

Now and again he has thought of this and that as offering some attraction, but his examination-work has been so absorbing that he has had no real opportunity to probe the matter to its depths. The opportunity has now arrived and he finds it something of a worry.

There is a pull here and a pull there.

The automobile Industry has advantages and disadvantages and just as he tries to weigh them impartially a friend recommends him the Stock Exchange; this goes through the same process, to be followed by importing, estate agency, insurance and the rest.

In this state of indecision, not to say drift, his mind has no focus and the power of interest is practically suspended except in the form of a desire to find a suitable calling.

Finally, the great decision is made and he resolves to go into banking. Instantly, all the powers of his mind are under the governance of a definite idea, the idea of becoming a banker.

His perceptions, his memory, his imagination, his judgment, his will, all the functions he can exercise act unitedly in the direction of his purpose.

We do not say that he never has a thought which is not connected with his work, let us hope he has for the sake of his sanity that he has, but that the one aim of his life gives his whole mind unity of action.

It fulfills the demand for a synthesis of abilities. In other words, he has set up a magnet in himself and good things begin to move in his direction. This is so obvious that it hardly needs attention and yet its importance is often overlooked:

1)   *Without a purpose we are sure to be drifters,* just going with the stream
2)   We work because we must, but when work is over we look around for something to pass the time
3)   *Life has no center*
4)   We are without a policy or a plan
5)   The effect is plain to the seeing eye, our abilities lose their edge and there comes a day when we realize that we are not what we once were

6)   We then get a glimpse of what we might have been

So it's obvious for us all now. We need a purpose, a plan.

1.5   Interest and Concentration

Concentration:

-       *"the effort to realize a purpose develops one of the
        specific functions of the mind, Concentration".*

We have dealt with hundreds of cases of mind-wandering and a very large percentage of them are just due to
aimlessness. Here is a specimen case:

"What is your trouble?" We ask our visitor.

"Well, when I sit down to do some figures or to read a
book, my mind won't stay on it, it runs away and at the
end of page I have to begin again. It is the same in
conversation. People talk to me and when they suddenly
ask 'Don't you think so yourself?' I don't know what they
refer to; my mind has drifted to something else".

We inquire as to how long this has been going on and
slowly get together the data of the case.

At last we come to the real question: "what would you
say is your particular aim in business, or in life?

Are you just jogging along or do you have a plan, an ambition?"

"Well, I reckon I'm just jogging along. I should like to increase my income, but it's easier said than done. As for ambition, that was knocked out of me years ago".

With this little revelation before us we proceed to show him how mind-wandering may be overcome, *mainly by reconstructing his own inner life in the service of a clear purpose* and partly by practice on approved lines.

He will set up a mental habit and instead of his thoughts flitting hither and thither without his knowing how or why, they will be focused on ways and means of increasing his efficiency and developing new ideas.

Further, a scheme of discipline, to be outlined later in the Course, will do wonders and in three months' time this self-distrustful man will tell us that he hardly knows himself: he could not have believed a cure could be for him so speedy and so effective.

1.6   The Folly of Overworking

Take a very different case, one in which a man's aim was clear, definite and intense.

But where it was too much for him.

He had three businesses slightly different in character:

From 9 to 10.30 a.m. he worked at number one.
From 10.30 a.m. to 1 p.m. he worked at number two.
From 1.30 p.m. to 7.30 p.m. he worked at number three.

Whilst at numbers one and two he had to think and act quickly; his brain worked at high pressure.

After two years of it he began to feel the lack of concentration; he had to read a letter twice to comprehend its meaning and he caught himself "wool-gathering" during most important interviews.

He admitted that he needed a rest. We just advised him something more drastic and told him that unless he cut down his working hours, not only now but for the future, he would become permanently enfeebled because:

1)   his purpose was too big
2)   the scheme was beyond his strength and
3)   the cause of his weakness lay in the consequent dissipation of his energy to an extent that made careful attention almost an impossibility

To have *"no aim is to drift"*; to have *"too many aims is to waste energy"*.

The Law of Interest is too clear to be misunderstood.

The deeper the interest, the stricter the attention.

The stricter the attention, the deeper the interest.

And as:

-   *"attention in the form of concentration means all the difference between great results and none at all"*,

the value of interest is fully demonstrated.

Interest begets Purpose *and* Purpose begets:

-   *"Concentration"*.

Sir William Hamilton declared that:

-   *"the difference between an ordinary mind and the mind of a Newton consists principally in this, that the one is capable of the application of a more continuous attention than the other..."*.

This is, in fact, what Sir Isaac, with equal modesty and shrewdness, himself admitted.

To one who complimented him on his genius he replied that if he had made any discoveries it was owing more to patient attention than to any other talent".

1.7   Interest and Memory

Memory:

-    *"the pursuit of a Purpose, of an Aim, of a Life-Goal*
     develops our Recollective Ability".

The power of Memory has the same story to tell about the value of purpose and interest.

The young law student who hopes soon to be called to the Bar pursues his study with zest. He desires very fervently to pass his examinations; hence, being interested, he aims at mastery and the difficulties of understanding and recollection tend rapidly to disappear.

Were he otherwise influenced, or indifferent, not caring whether he was successful or not, he would read his law books with a wandering mind, attention would be weak and therefore memory would be indistinct, unready and unreliable.

Look back in your life and ask yourself:

-    *"what are the thoughts and things*
     that I remember most vividly?"

You will find they are the thoughts and things happy or unhappy that were emotionally experienced.

Here is an extract from a correspondent's letter, illustrating this statement:

"The three facts I remember best are a case of a pal being drowned before my eyes; I nearly went under myself; a case of sudden mental elevation on a Swiss mountain and a case of utter astonishment during my first peep through an observatory telescope".

1.8   Memory and Emotion

Pain-memories are outside our purview.

We are dealing with a form of pleasure-memory which is associated with some plan, aim or purpose that lies near our heart.

Is it not clear that the details of a study, of a business, of a profession, or any enterprise in which we are interested will be far more easily remembered than details toward which we are either indifferent or hostile?

We were interviewing a young man of twenty-five who complained of weak memory for business matters, such as posting letters, telephone messages, dates and orders.

But we found he knew practically everything about football, dates of matches, names of teams, professionals and the exact results of play.

About these matters he was a walking encyclopedia.

His heart was in football, not in business and:

- *"where your heart is there is your memory also".*

Memory, however, may be weakened while interest remains unimpaired.

There is the sick man, for instance, who, whether a student, a merchant, or a doctor, is certain to have a weaker memory during illness than when in health, even though interest-power is normally well-developed.

There are also those cases in which shock, overwork or some other cause has brought about an eccentricity in the recollective powers.

The stages are now as follows:

- *"Interest => Purpose => Concentration => Memory".*

Or, as Dr. Johnson puts it:

- *"attention is the mother of memory and interest is the mother of attention. To secure memory, secure both her mother and her grandmother".*

Is there a further development? Yes.

1.9   Interest and Ideation

The further development is:

-       *"there is an increase in the Fertility of Ideas"*.

It has been our good fortune to have the opportunity to study the records of genius and in almost every case we have found that the originalities and discoveries of great men have been due primarily to this impulse, to a feeling or emotion that passes easily from a state of interest into a plan of action.

Let one instance suffice.

Finsen, the celebrated light-cure specialist, saw a cat reclining lazily on a roof in the genial sunshine.

The shadow from a neighboring building reached the cat and it moved into the sunshine again.

It repeated the process several times.

Finsen became interested and his interest deepened and widened with attention to the subject. He knew the cat must have received some benefit from the light and heat, but how and why? At last he felt himself on the track of a great discovery and eventually his new ideas found their expression in the famous Finsen cure.

You will perhaps say: Is not this a case where attention developed interest rather than the other way about?

No. Finsen became interested in the movements of the cat and this interest caused a concentration on the why and wherefore of the whole affair. We shall later on deal with the interest that springs out of attention.

1.10   Genius and Concentration

It is remarkable how confident many writers have been and still are: *"that genius with all its glories is due to concentration in some form",* instead of to some ability that is altogether superior to the ability of even a talented mind:

1)   Buffon said that *"genius is no more than great patience"*
2)   Helvetius said it was *"only prolonged attention"*
3)   Matthew Arnold said it was *"mainly an affair of energy"*

But these are only half-truths. The whole truth is this:

-   *"attention, reflection, energy, mental-industry, prepare the conditions of our own originality"* and

-   *"the new idea is the off-spring of the subconscious sphere of intellect".*

That is why the new idea "comes", it makes its appearance *suddenly*, when, perhaps, the mind is engaged on something quite different.

Still, the value of attention is not diminished: rather it is increased.

1.11   The Growth of Ideas

With your powers of interest working at a high but not abnormal pressure, your ideas will grow in number and quality, because you will always be inquiring into the origins and relationships of your business, profession, or calling, as well as into those that are external to it.

Clerk-Maxwell showed that a repeated electrical or magnetic disturbance, or change, would set up and radiate waves of an electro-magnetic nature in the ether.

And Clerk-Maxwell showed also that, with some specific assumptions concerning the ether, these waves would travel with the velocity of light.

Upon this is based his electro-magnetic theory of light.

The experimental proof of this theorem was made by Hertz, who produced very rapidly oscillating electric currents by means of sparks between the plates of a condenser.

Marconi then became interested and in his turn began to experiment in order to test some ideas of practical use which deep reflection had brought to him.

In this way came the great wireless system as we know it.

Once more it is:

-       "Interest leads to Attention"

-       "Attention leads to Memory" and

-       "Memory leads to Ideas".

To summarize then, the total outcome of Interest is:

1)   Attention Power
2)   Concentration Power
3)   Emotional Power
4)   Memory Power
5)   Fertility of Ideas
6)   Self Confidence
7)   Will-Power

We have seven different steps right here which influence each other.

From a didactic perspective we have put these seven steps again in a scheme on the next page.

1.12   The 7 steps of the Process of Interest in a scheme

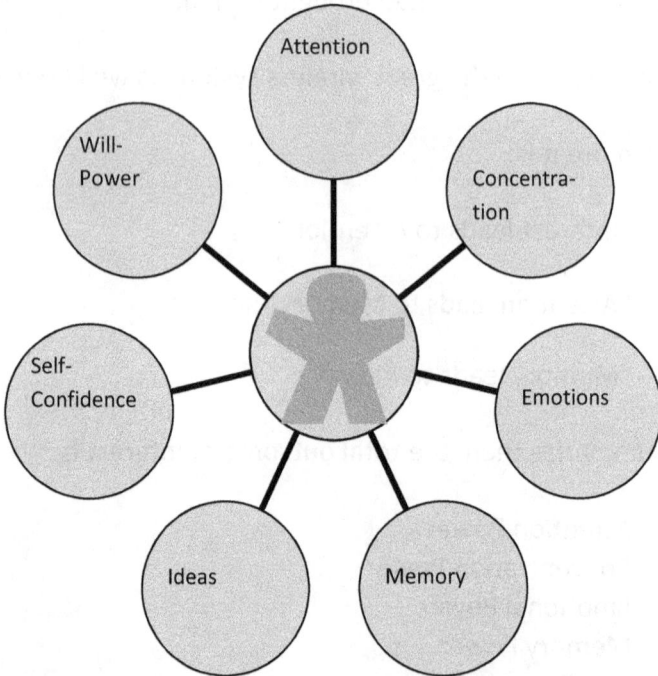

Explanation:

In this chapter 1 we talked a lot about the importance of interest. As you can see above interest has seven special effects. It leads to attention, concentration, emotions, memory, ideas, self-confidence and will-power.

CHAPTER 2: Your Purpose in Life

CHAPTER 2:   Your Purpose in Life

Looking for your Purpose in Life is that what it's all about?

2.1   Stimulus

Have you not heard A say of B: "I wonder where he gets all his ideas?" It is a remark with some grudge and envy in it.

A has done his best and yet B always excels him. Why?

Probably because B has a cleverer brain, or has gone through a course of training, or works harder.

But it is equally probable that A has not the same a-mount of stimulus as B and that when he is on the same level in this respect, he will be equal to B's output of ideas both in quality and quantity.

We often have been astonished at the exceedingly clever manner in which quite uneducated men have managed a business, or organized a campaign where considerable is-sues were involved.

True, they have bungled a few things where precision of utterance and fineness of taste were needed, but the es-sential ideas were involved and carried out with real great and astonishing executive power.

These men had *force* and it arose from the enthusiasm they possessed for the work in hand.

Apply these facts to your own affairs. Why are you sometimes destitute of ideas? There are two reasons:

1) A stagnant period, long or short, nearly always follows a creative period; a season of mental plenty is succeeded by one of comparative poverty. That is *"intellectual rhythm"*: a point to which, so far as we are aware, attention has not elsewhere been explicitly drawn in this connection.
2) But the more serious reason is this: that the fires of interest have died down. You have lost force. Results are fewer. Attention, generally, is slacker. Concentration weakens.

The cure is obvious:

- *"increase the stimulus and ideas will come"*.

The law of stimulus has been formulated in the following words:

- *"the efficiency of a feeling, as a motive power, is determined by its intensity and by its duration"*.

Your interest must be permanent and it must be strong; otherwise you gain nothing.

If

1) You are a changeable person, one week enthusiastic about this or that and the next week as cold as ice

2) Your interest, though permanent, has not enough steam behind it: its force is irregular

The habit of intensity must be acquired. This brings us to a point the fuller treatment of which we must postpone till we come, in one of the next paragraphs, to the more precise consideration of the nature of Will-Power.

2.2 Interest and Self-Confidence

Interest Power:

- *"interest-power, when expressed in action, is one of the bases of complete Self-Confidence".*

As this is matter of extreme importance, we propose to investigate it now fully. At first, *what is meant by Self-Confidence?* The dictionary defines it as:

- *"trust in one's own strength, or powers; relying on the correctness of one's own judgment, or the com-petence of one's own powers, without other aid".*

No one is *absolutely* lacking in this desirable quality of mind and character; there is generally one sphere, usually our business or profession, where we are at home and concerning which we speak and act without self-mistrust.

A shoemaker may be painfully shy in social life and altogether lacking in initiative in public affairs, but if you venture to criticize his opinions about leather, he may end by saying that you talk like a fool.

"We are all of us confident enough when we know and we usually do know something about our own Calling".

A boy at school may know the right answer but he is too shy to speak. When he becomes a man the habit is still there and although he has the knowledge and ability to advance his interests, he always hangs back.

This is because his temperament is *reserved*. He secretly longs to push ahead, but he hates the pushing spirit; consequently, the more assertive man gets ahead of him.

2.3   How Temperament Affects Us

Temperament, therefore, often stands in the way of a certain kind of progress, especially in all circumstances where competition rules.

Occasionally it happens that the cleverest men are in the second and third positions and the average men in the first.

But these average men are superior in one particular:

-       *"they are of an energetic and
        self-confident disposition"*.

They are not to be blamed for this; neither are the others to be blamed because a sense of reserve prevents them from taking part in the struggle of competitive life.

We do not want to see a world chuck full of *"climbers"* who desire nothing but selfish advantage. Neither do we desire to see hundreds of persons who are too timid to strike out for themselves.

We duly appreciate the value of the reserved temperament, as seen in the life and work of many an idealist and are not blind to the merits of men of energy, who calmly take up the responsibilities of leadership.

But if a man of hesitant mind desires to enter the sphere in which he must pit his abilities against those of other men, he cannot expect the rules of the game to be altered to suit his convenience. He must accept the position as he finds it and go in and win.

In doing so he need not cease to be a gentleman. Just as in the tense struggle of a boat race, we see mind and muscle pitted against mind and muscle in the spirit of true sportsmanship, so on any plane of human life there may be healthy rivalry conducted on the basis of the highest honor.

Should a man follow his temperament, or adjust it to his needs? That is a question which no one can decide except the man himself.

It has been said that there are men who by no possible agency could change their mental tendencies from deep reserve to forceful activity: we have known scores of others who have succeeded in so doing. By nature they were retiring and contemplative, but by personal decision they became active, almost pugnacious.

But there is a sense in which *"Interest-Power can bring more action and vim into any life"* and adapt a policy of progress to every temperament.

For instance, an interest in the subject of slavery and a desire to abolish it in every form, brought many men and women of reserved temperament into the sphere of action during the nineteenth century.

In some cases the action consisted of:

1)   writing books and pamphlets
2)   in others it took the form of lectures and
3)   in the energetic folk, it was seen in their vigorous political campaigns

All temperaments were affected and all expressed themselves accordingly.

2.4   The Place of Knowledge in Self-Confidence

Now your interest may be, probably is, much less ambitious than the abolition of a great evil, but if it is intense, it will surely find opportunities of expression.

And even if your temperament is an obstacle, changes will occur tending to reduce the opposition, perhaps to banish it altogether:

1)   In this way self-confidence is developed
2)   You know your subject, or you are getting to know it
3)   And, the natural desire to hold back is giving way to experience

Let there be no mistake. If you really resolve to master a timid disposition, you *can*. How is it to be done?

By arousing some Feeling in the form of Desire and by expressing it in some definite aim.

Your self-respect demands that when you go before a superior to ask a favor you shall not stammer out your words and knock your knees together. Say to yourself: *"This sort of thing must stop. It is not dignified"*.

At first the old feeling will return, however strong the resolution, but it gradually weakens.

2.5   A Barrie Illustration

A student once wrote to us, saying that there were cases where self-confidence in the sense of *"relying on one's own judgment"* may be seriously at fault and he sent us an entertaining case by way of illustration. Here it is.

Sir James Barrie had a project from Mr. Charles Froham to write a play and when he delivered the manuscript to Froham he said:

-    *"I am sure it will not be a commercial success, but it is a dream child of mine and I am so anxious to see it on the stage that I have written another play which I shall be glad to give you and which will compensate you for any loss of the one I am so eager to have produced".*

"Do not trouble about that", said Froham, *"I will produce both plays".*

Now the extraordinary thing about this episode is, that the play about whose success he was so doubtful was *"Peter Pan"*. It made several fortunes. The manuscript he offered Froham to indemnify him from loss was *"Alice Sit-by-the-fire"*, which lasted only a season.

Such is the estimate that the author often puts on his own work.

This is extremely interesting in itself.

But if Sir James Barrie had just been lacking in the Self-Confidence we are talking about, he would have said to Froham:

- *"I really can't write a play for you, not one that's good enough. I mistrust my own powers".*

Instead of putting it in that way he produced two *plays*, one of which he felt sure would compensate for the losses of the other, whose money-bringing power he doubted, nor its literary and human qualities, for it was a *"dream child"*, which an author treasures above every-thing else.

Thus Barrie was not lacking in self-confidence: *"he was simply mistaken in estimating the box-office value of a new play"*.

Now Interest-Power, as we have seen already, gives:

1)   the mind unity of action
2)   it also leads to concentration and other develop-ments and
3)   out of these come trust and confidence

A man feels he can do certain things when called upon, because he *"has prepared himself"* to do them and has succeeded. This feeling of great confidence, shown in one sphere, has a tendency to pass over to other spheres.

And, he who trusts himself thoroughly in his business or profession, realizes that the same power can be obtained in other and new directions, simply because he has faith in his abilities, generated by enthusiasm and tested by his own experience.

2.6   Interest and Will-Power

There is a final benefit to be considered:

-      *"Interest increases Will-Power"*.

The thing you want to do with *all your heart*, because you believe it is a good thing to do, advantageous to you and to all the others, is the thing: *"about which you will have no difficulty as to take action"*.

Your *"enthusiasm"* will carry you through.

Though you find you have to work early and late you will do it.

This fact is one of the simplicities of mental life, but its importance is often not realized.

Those men who find themselves languid, indifferent, lazy or unresponsive, are usually men:

1) without an interest
2) therefore without a purpose
3) without concentration
4) and without will

It is a case of cause and effect and every psychologist has told us about it in plain words.

We do not deny that there are other aspects of the relationship, but here we confine our attention to the interest which has an end in view and which develops all-round mental ability by the effort to attain it.

Part of that ability is, necessarily, power of Will.

But that Will has its first origin in the feeling of interest and not only its origin but its continued sustenance, so that the exercise of Will-Power shall become a *"habit"*.

So if you one day feel that your Will is weak, despite good health and the absence of anxiety, just go back to your real purpose in living and examine it to see whether it retains its original compelling force:

1) Are you as eager as you were?
2) Or, has life lost its savor?

In most instances it will be found that weak Will is due to:

1) loss of impetus, or stimulus
2) desire has decreased
3) concentration is not so strong

All these things are intimately connected and although there are other factors which cannot be ignored, the chief factor *is* Interest.

There can be no doubt that the *habit* of overcoming difficulties in the attainment of a life-ambition will exert a healthy reflex influence throughout the whole mind.

A man who conquers *here* will be apt to conquer *there*.

But not necessarily.

We have known men who possessed great strength of will in business.

But were without any resolution at all in other departments of life, in which it was often badly needed.

2.7   The 7 aspects of establishing Your Purpose in Life

If we want to be successful in life and if we want to realise our Purpose in Life we need to give attention to the following seven aspects.

These seven aspects are:

1) Desire / Stimulus / Purpose
2) Interest
3) Self-Confidence
4) Temperament
5) Knowledge
6) Action
7) Will-Power

We have 7 different steps which influence each other.

The most important step is the first of course.

We all need a stimulus, a desire or a purpose to explore our possibilities in full in our private life as in our business life as well.

So just start.

What is your heart longing for at this moment?

What is your greatest desire ever? What is your message to this society and to your friends and family?

Don't wait until you found the 100% perfect answer. Just start and you will see what will happen in your life.

You will be very surprised.

2.8   The 7 aspects of Your Purpose in Life in a scheme

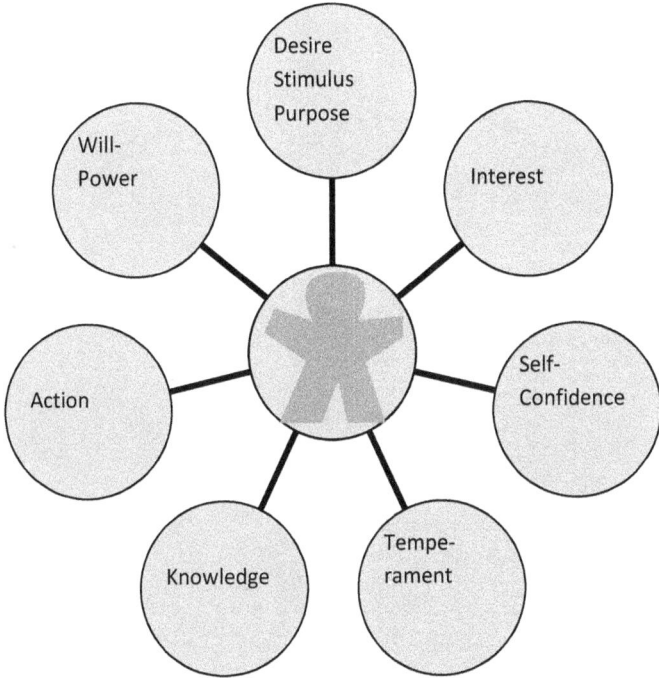

Desire
Stimulus
Purpose

Will-
Power

Interest

Action

Self-
Confidence

Knowledge

Tempe-
rament

Explanation:

In this chapter 2 we talked about the importance of a right stimulus, to have a great desire and to work and live with a special focus and purpose. The ultimate goal is to improve your Will-Power so you can achieve your goals.

CHAPTER 3: How to Get an Aim

CHAPTER 3:   How to Get an Aim

We are sometimes asked the fair question: *"how can I obtain an interest in life and form a plan of action?"*

Now before that very reasonable question can be answered, we must know something about the person who asks it.

A wife and mother, for instance, has already a mission to accomplish and nothing can be higher than the proper training of children in the principles of right living. She may, however, wish to develop her mental abilities in order to be the companion of her children when they grow up and begin to think for themselves. In that case the aim is made still more clear and definite.

Not a few people of both sexes may be found among our students, whose *"general purpose"* in the world, so far as business or profession is concerned, may be regarded as fixed, but there are certain auxiliary aims open to them which may be included under the heading of a broader mental culture.

3.1   What Is an Aim?

Before we consider other classes of people to whom the decision of an aim in life is a difficulty, let us critically examine the phrase itself.

What is an Aim?

1)   It does not necessarily mean *a great mission*
2)   It may mean no more than doing well, or doing better, the work you are doing now

A miner may believe that he has no aim in life, for getting coal is merely work, whereas an aim, he thinks, is a vast ambition:

-    *"such as to own a mine or become a Minister of Labor".*

He may be right or wrong, so far as he himself is concerned, but it is practical wisdom to have an *immediate* purpose as well as a *distant* one.

And in the miner's case, the obtaining of a sound education might be the primary object of life.

Do not, therefore, imagine that aims must be dizzy ambitions; they are much more modest than that and their value does not lie in their *height* so much as just in their *"intensity"*.

When one purpose has been achieved it is comparatively easy to form another, for effort has brought experience and decisions have a better chance of being intelligently adapted to one's abilities.

3.2   The two Rules to be Followed

At this point we come in contact with the serious question of vocational choice.

For, obviously, a man's aim in life and the interest which is connected with it, should be largely influenced by his aptitude for some particular line of work.

The two rules to be followed are these:

1) if you are not in the right job, keep working at it industriously until you find the right one
2) never let go with one hand until you have gripped with the other

3.3   Some Cases Considered

Men and women who have assured incomes do not need an aim or purpose which concerns itself with earning bread and butter; their plans are consequently connected with reading, education, social service, Church work or politics. The nature of the avocation does not affect the question in the least:

- *"any sort of interest power that is of a worthy character will tend to bring out the hidden possibilities of mind"*, as well as to develop its more obvious powers.

Again, professional men may be said to possess already sufficient directive influence to satisfy the claims of interest and purpose.

They are clergymen, lawyers, surveyors, doctors, editors or accountants, but it often happens that although the general nature of their destiny is decided, the *particular* element in it is not.

A doctor may have resolved to be a doctor always, but what kind of a doctor?

- a specialist?
- a specialist in what branch?
- a general practitioner?
- a surgeon?
- a medical author?

In which direction does interest lead him? When that question is decided, he can, after due reflection, begin to formulate plans of action.

There are thousands of persons whose general future is settled, but who have no particular interest beyond the daily round and common task.

Some of them look on their calling as a necessary labor, but also as a nuisance and they live their real life at home among books, or specimens, or flowers.

Such people often live long, happy and useful lives, but it cannot always be said of them that they have made the best of their possibilities.

If the business fails or hard times come, they frequently pass through the deep waters of suffering, experiences which a true mental attitude towards work would either have spared them altogether, or have enabled them to endure with courage and keeping up with a strong mind.

3.4 When Purpose Is *"Discovered"*

There is still another difficulty in connection with the formulation of a personal purpose. We can best explain it by saying that in some cases the life purpose, the selection of a calling or a line of action wherein enthusiasm is possible, is arrived at only after repeated efforts, extending, it may be, over a number of years.

A young man, let us suppose, finds himself in the Department of Public Treasury at Washington, D.C.

He was told the Civil Service was a good thing and no doubt in many respects this is true, but he soon begins to kick against the routine.

All the while he is restless: he has a hemmed-in feeling, and his friends advise him this way and that until he is utterly confused.

One day, if he is of literary bent and has always most readily devoted his leisure to literature, he yields to the stirrings of inspiration.

He discovers that the more he draws upon it the more copious is the stream of his ideas.

With practice he develops a method and style of his own. A manuscript is accepted.

After a while he realizes that he has found his true vocation in life and soon the resounding corridors of Washington, D.C. know him no more.

He is an author now and for always.

But his bent might have been mathematical and ultimately he would have found himself in an Insurance Office as an Actuary. Such cases are bewildering in their number and variety. Lord Reading's actual start in life was on the Stock Exchange; the real purpose was in the law and diplomacy.

In all spheres of work there are cases where men and women, do not really live their full lives until the passing of time has brought the right opportunity.

So we counsel *"patience"*, believing that in the majority of instances the true calling will be found.

"But", it may be urged, *"will not mental ability decline during the aimless period?"*

Not if a man is doing the best he knows.

His powers will deteriorate, no doubt, if he allows himself to drift, to become cynical, or despairing.

There is always work to be done and to aim at excellence while doing it is to keep the feelings active and the mind alert. Naturally, the advent of a clear-cut aim, with a forceful interest in control, will make a vast difference.

3.5   Self-Realization

A consideration of what has been said ought just to leave every reader cheerful and confident.

You may have had:

1)   your aim, clear and unmistakable, before you took up this book or
2)   you may have received from it just the kind of guidance you needed to help you in formulating your plan or
3)   you may still be undecided

But in no case should there be anything akin to dismay and hopelessness.

Summarized:

1)   *If you know what you want,* this book and those
      which follow, will promote every interest you have
      at heart

2)   *If you do not know what you want,* you know at any
      rate that the needed knowledge will come and that,
      for the present, you can go forward with a heart full
      of great expectancy

So dispense with the pessimism which tempts you all the
time to believe that the world is against you!

Thrust aside the cynicism which says progress is the special mirage created for the delectation of fools.

As well as the song of luck which affirms that all life's
benefits are bestowed by the luck of chance!

In a universe governed by law there is a sense in which
man alone is a law unto himself.

He is, indeed, a point upon which many forces converge
in accordance with the laws which govern them.

But, he alone, with the resources he has at his command,
is capable of modifying his reactions to their impact in
accordance with his own highest interests. He alone is
able to set his life-goals in private as in business as well.

Take yourself in hand and resolve that in spite of every difficulty you will *"arrive",* not in the limelight of public opinion but in the sense of *"self-realization"*.

3.6   Failure and Half-Success

Saint Paul as he approached the end of his historic career and looked back, said:

-    *"I have fought the good fight".*

It was a reflection based on acts and sufferings to which he was urged by an overpowering force of conviction.

Many men, towards the end, are obliged to say:

- "I have wasted my time on unessentials"
- "I have missed the substance to embrace the shadow"
- "I have allowed most men to leave me behind"
- "I have not come up to the expectations of my friends and have rejoiced my enemies"
- "I have sought the easy line in all things"
- "I have not quite failed but my success has been insignificant"

It is not too late to arrange a plan of life that shall make such confessions impossible in your case. But begin the arranging *now*. Don't lose a day.

Elderly students, who have enrolled for the purpose of restoring waning powers and of maintaining them in full vigor, occupy a position special to themselves.

The main object of life has long been settled.

It has been pursued without success or just with partial success, or is already on the way to automatic realization.

Let them change a little their point of view, their mental attitude.

Let them bring imagination into play for the revival of their pristine zest and they will renew their grip upon life.

The slackening of which they were conscious will give place to keenness and the feeling of weakness will yield to growing confidence.

CHAPTER 4:   Causes of Aimless Lives

CHAPTER 4:   Causes of Aimless Lives

Among the chief causes responsible for a lack of aim are these:

1)   an absence of training in early initiative
2)   a shy and reserved temperament, predisposing to inaction
3)   the after-effects of nervous illnesses
4)   a native changeability of disposition, no power of concentrated effort
5)   weakness of will, causing disinclination to effort
6)   a profession or business chosen without sufficient reference to ability or aptitude, which therefore denies just full scope for self-expression for yourself
7a)   pessimism: sometimes arising out of a deep study of one aspect of life, which has culminated in too many negatives thought by the person involved
7b)   fatalism: which regards the individual as the help-less victim of circumstances, as a mere point upon which forces converge, whereas he is himself *"a force capable of"* resisting, restraining, compelling

Perhaps you are beginning to think it desirable to exchange your occupation for another.

Such a change should not be attempted unless in exceptional circumstances and with a reasonable prospect of betterment.

4.1   The 7 Causes of Aimless Lives in a scheme

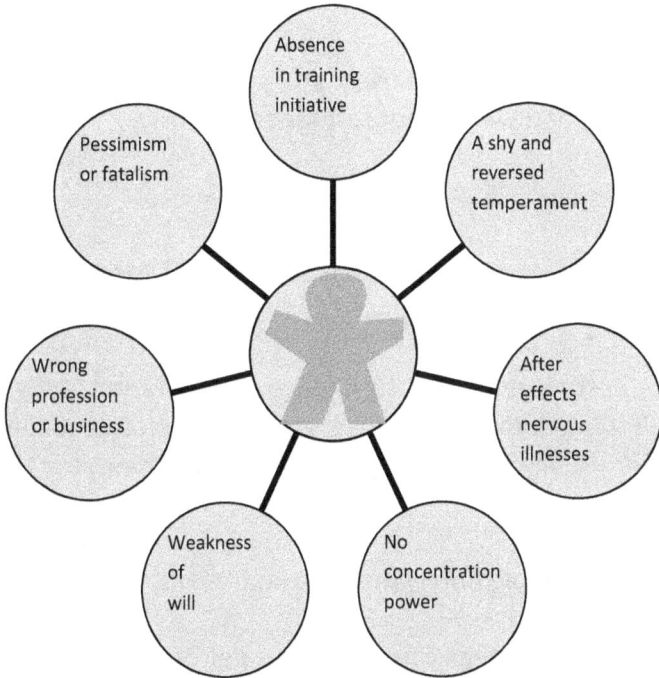

Explanation:

As we can see above, we have 7 serious causes of Aimless Lives and it's quite a great job not to fall in one of these seven all over the years when you grow up. A right desire, a good stimulus and a great purpose will help you a lot.

Before you release your hold on the rope which is supporting you, make sure that your clutch of the new rope is firm and sure.

And see that when you leave you carry with you the respect and good will of your former employers.

4.2   Decision *versus* Indecision

As a rule, the necessity of earning a living causes the majority to choose a calling.

If not hastily, yet with little chance of adaptation and as a result we get the round pegs in square holes, but these people usually have one great advantage mentally: *they know what they want*.

The other people don't; they are undecided.

Now the round pegs can very often get out of the square holes if they play their part with caution and skill. In their leisure time they can prepare themselves for new work and new positions and, when ready, can migrate and better themselves.

4.3   Change of Environment

In some communities or circumstances it is possible for a man to change his occupation without prejudice.

This is particularly so in new countries where class distinctions are not marked and where the conditions of life and work demand active intelligence, initiative and some adaptability rather than specialization.

A change even from one town to another has the effect of widening the range of consciousness, sharpening the vision and removing those inhibitions that make us hesitant and subconscious in seeking new kinds of work in our old surroundings and among old acquaintances.

A change of environment often means a change of outlook.

For not only are our eyes freshened to observe new things or to find in old things a new interest, but we ourselves are judged without preconceptions.

The newcomer is always an object of interest.

Sometimes it is not necessary to go to another country or town to fresh up your mind and to sharpen your vision. You can look by yourself for some new experiences by:

- visits to different parts of the town in which you live
- visits to different restaurants, contact with people of different modes of life and thought
- the analysis of businesses and industries different from that in which you are engaged

All these experiences will enlarge your knowledge of men and women and of affairs and bring you into touch with favorable opportunities.

Such practices will diminish self-consciousness and give you standards of comparison that will enable you better to understand yourself.

If you are preparing yourself for better work and have a definite aim, *"your magnet"* will do the rest.

4.4   The Voice of the Cynic

We have heard the cynic say*:*

-    *"why should* everyone *have an aim or a purpose?"*

Why not have a few people who are without these things for the sake of contrast?

This is as much as to say:

-    *"why should* everybody *be honest?"*

Why not have a few thieves and rogues by way of variety?

We *have* them, unfortunately. Life is an imperfect affair and the contrasts will always be in evidence.

But the true reply to the cynic is this:

-    *"success in achieving an aim lies more in the educative power of making the effort than in the actual achievement itself"*.

Nearly all healthy people love progressive movement *"for its own sake"*, not merely for what is at the end of it.

They revel in the thrill of ideas that transform.

4.5   Testing an Aim

You can gauge the real quality of an aim by asking the following 7 questions:

1)   Is its achievement desirable?
2)   Is it possible or impossible?
3)   Is it possible or impossible to *me*?
4)   What are the obstacles?
5)   Can they be surmounted?
6)   Will victory be too costly?
7)   Can I find any happiness in the effort if it fails?

These 7 questions to test the quality of an aim are put in a scheme again on the following page. As we have seen above: the most important part of achieving an aim is the fun of the road.

4.6   The 7 Questions to Test the Quality of an Aim

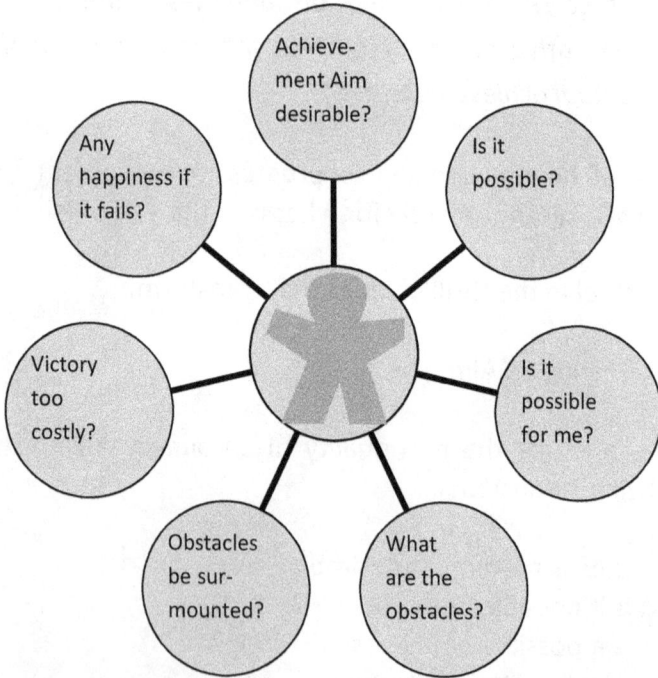

Explanation:

As we can see above, we have 7 questions to test the real quality of an Aim. Most important part is the fun on the road. For example; you can write a play, most of the fun is in writing it. Happiness will succeed if the play is played.

4.7   Introspection It's Use and Abuse

There can be no doubt that in order to make this course a success, you will have to examine yourself closely, to turn your attention inward and use for a while the searchlight of introspection.

Some people are afraid of introspection. So are we:

-    *"when it is habitually indulged, without
     a definite purpose and for its own sake"*.

To encourage this habitual looking within is the last thing we desire and the whole trend of this course is toward an outside interest, an interest where one is not conscious of self.

4.8   Self-Consciousness

Perhaps it will not be amiss at this juncture to say a word about the evil of self-consciousness. Take a simple illus-tration.

You are suddenly called upon to second a vote of thanks, or to say a few genial words at a dinner. You are not ac-customed to speech making and become unpleasantly self-conscious instead of thinking only about the subject and the occasion. Perhaps a hundred and twenty pairs of eyes look at you and you feel hypnotized.

You want to speak well and in order to estimate your success you feel obliged to listen to yourself as you talk.

There comes a moment when these two activities of speaking and listening do not run side by side.

You allow the listening too much scope and the speaking fails to get its due; that is the moment when a speaker loses the thread of his remarks and comes to a full stop.

Now, if you can forget yourself in the subject and the occasion, in other words, speak without listening critically, you will find yourself much more fluent.

We have known self-conscious people who have delivered thrilling speeches, the reason being that they were supremely anxious to advocate the claims of a particular cause that was very close to their hearts and the desire completely overcame the habit of thinking of self.

"They forgot themselves" in the passion of the moment and self was lost in the glow and fervor of speaking for a great object.

Of course self-consciousness is often *"temperamental"*:

-   *"even a very self-confident man may be painfully embarrassed if suddenly called upon to speak before a great audience".*

People who are naturally shy and reserved have a tendency to live a good deal within themselves.

And being sensitive, the rough and tumble of everyday life, the chaff and the joking, the give-and-take of social existence, does not attract them: indeed, such people try to avoid everything that would jar their inward peace.

Whether they know it or not, they must be told that there is a little vanity in their attitude.

However much they shrink from publicity it is not all due to fear.

They should realize that a healthy balance of life requires a man to come out of his reserve; otherwise he becomes so self-conscious that he stands in his own light, hinders his progress and increases other people's pity toward him.

The one way to do this is to:

1)   develop an interest
2)   form a plan for carrying it out and
3)   concentrate upon it

This, with such social recreation as life usually offers, will suffice in time to cure the evil, even if it exists in a radical form.

4.9   A Specimen of Self-Examination

To return to introspection. Occasional practice of it for a definite purpose is the chief method of self-knowledge.

For instance, here is a practical question:

-    *"do you possess energy or impelling force?"*

To test yourself once and thoroughly on that basis, is to obtain encouragement if you can say: "Yes".

Illumination and guidance if you have to say: "No".

Let us take a few negative answers:

1)   "No. No energy. I'm like an icicle. I am cold, lacking in broad sympathies, frigid and incapable of any enthusiasm"
2)   "I have some energy, but only as a routinist. I allow others to do my thinking. I render obedience because I never had the force to lead. I am essentially an employed person"
3)   "Yes, I've got energy for short periods. But I'm like a Seidlitz powder. I fizz and foam with enthusiasm for awhile, then fall as flat as ditch water"

There is more hope for men who know themselves, than for men who have never faced an honest self-analysis.

Provided steps are taken to turn the knowledge to good account:

- *"to lament one's defects and to do nothing to remedy them is fatal".*

The courage demanded in self-examination is to "see all and not to be afraid".

And it should be followed by equal courage in setting your mental house in order.

Like Mr. Britling, you must "see it through".

Research has provided that there is a relationship between intelligence and the ability to judge oneself.

Thus, the answering of the following Self-drill questions should be self-revealing in a new and interesting manner.

4.10   Questions for Self-Drill

1)   Are you thoroughly sound physically? If not, are you taking suitable steps for the improvement of your health?

2)   Do you find that the knowledge of some weakness stimulates you to fresh energy in order to compensate for the defect? Is this true of mental as well as physical defects?

3) Have you ever examined your mental qualities in comparison with those of other people, for whose success, intellectual, social, or commercial, you may have felt an occasional pang of envy? If so, with what result?

4) What were the most successful and happy periods of your life? Do your best and most progressive periods synchronize with your best health periods?

5) Can you now reproduce the mental and other conditions of those successful periods in order to obtain similar results?

6) If there have been no such periods do you blame yourself? If not, can you blame anyone else, fairly?

7) Have you discovered what, for yourself, is the best hour for calm reflection, the sort of reflection that leads to advantageous action?

8) Draw up a list of your good qualities and those which you would classify as not so good.

9) What is your remote or distant aim, also your more immediate aim?

10) Are you too sensitive, too retiring? If so, do you not lose much in consequence?

11) Have you proved the truth of the statement that for success in anything, the usual program is *continuous* hard work?

12) Do you welcome responsibility? Do you realize how the acceptance of responsibility contributes to the development of mind and the making of character?

13) Lavater says: *"there are three classes of men: the retrograde, the stationary and the progressive"*. To which do you belong?

14) When you left school, or college, did you keep up a plan of formal study, or did you simply *"let things go?"*

15) Do you perform any kind of work for others where financial reward is out of the question? Do you recognize a moral obligation to pay your benefactors by benefiting others as you have an opportunity? How long is it since you did something really kind and generous?

16) Have you made the production of new ideas a definite aim? Or, have you been content just to accept other people's ideas with a *"thank you"* for saving you the trouble?

17) Do you waste energy by:

   (a) imagining misfortunes and how you would meet them?
   (b) by going through imaginary battles with your enemies?
   (c) by thinking pessimistic thoughts on general lines?

If the use of these Self-Drill questions has depressed you.

Is it not because they have shown you where your weakness lies?

Is not that a hopeful thing inasmuch as you can begin at once to provide a remedy?

We attach great importance to these Self-Drill questions. Not as questions only.

But as a means of organizing your energies.

Don't skip them.

Don't say they are for others and not for you:

- *"if your life is not advancing, it is probably because there is some lack of plan which the Self-Drill questions will discover".*

4.11   Concluding Reflections

Having now surveyed the whole position, the next step for the student is to:

1)   gather together all the facts which relate to his possible future
2)   when these are assembled, it becomes his duty to *value* them and that is, to place them in their order of importance
3)   finally, he must come to a conclusion and
4)   begin a line of action accordingly

All this usually calls for serious and careful attention, the exceptions being those cases in which the future is already, or nearly, decided. Your own case may have its peculiarities, due to individual idiosyncrasies and to factors in local conditions.

The adjustment of these requires close scrutiny and a good deal of patience.

Do not make a too hasty and hurried decision on such important matter.

Consider everything germane to the position you want: deep interest, adequate ability, endurance, expenses, income, prospects and so forth.

If you cannot see your way ahead, if nothing takes shape after long inquiry and reflection, do not despair:

-       *"the man who develops his own powers and aims at excellence, has something good coming his way".*

He will arrive eventually even though by a circuitous route.

4.12   Conclusion of defining a real Life Aim

So if we make a short summary of chapter 4 we come to the following conclusion.

To come to a real Life Aim we need the following seven prior conditions and knowledge:

1)　Did you make a decision yet?
2)　Is a change of environment needed?
3)　Do you have the right mental attitude?
4)　Did you test your Aim with the 7 questions in this chapter already?
5)　Did you do some introspection to value your qualities, your powers, your talents and your capacities?
6)　Do you possess the required energy to do the job?
7)　Are you focused day by day at your Aim?

The seven aspects of having a real Life Aim are:

1)　Do you possess the right energy?
2)　Do you have a deep interest?
3)　Do you have the adequate ability?
4)　Do you have the required endurance?
5)　What are the expected expenses?
6)　What is the expected income?
7)　Do you have any prospects yet?

We have put above in the following two schemes. As we will see the whole process starts with making a decision and a right mental attitude and energy is also required, but most important of all is focus. The focus to succeed and to aim permanently at your life-goal.

4.13   The 7 Prior Conditions of Having a Real Life Aim

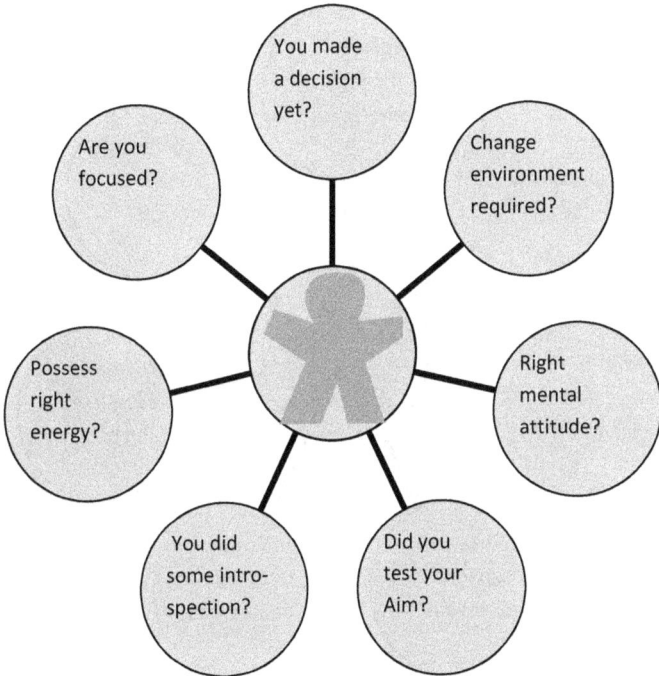

Explanation:

As we can see above, we have 7 prior conditions to set for having a real Life Aim. Of course the whole process starts with making a decision and a right mental attitude and energy is also required, but most important of all is focus.

4.14   The 7 Aspects of Having a Real Life Aim

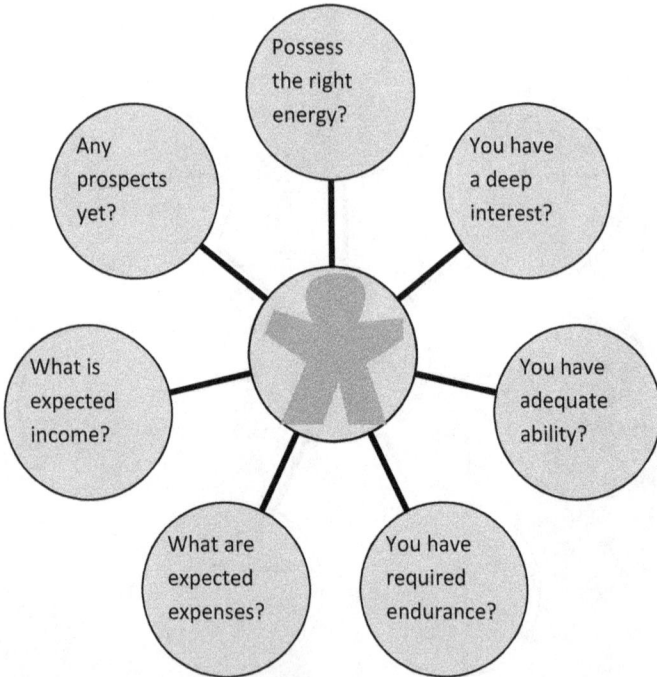

Explanation:

As we can see above, we have 7 aspects of fulfilling your real dream in life. It starts with the required energy of course and interest, adequate abilities and endurance are the most important aspects regarding to this subject now.

CHAPTER 5: Memory Training

CHAPTER 5:   Memory Training

Right now a few characteristics of our memory will be dealt with. A good memory will brighten up your future.

5.1   The Cost of Forgetfulness

Forgetfulness is both irritating and costly in any sphere of life and this is particularly true in the world of business:

- you miss an appointment and lose a big contract
- you forget to show a customer a certain line of goods and lose an order
- you arrive on the spot without material or some necessary implement
- you decide to go fishing without the bait, as the saying goes

Forgetfulness has exacted a heavy toll in human lives and a still heavier toll in money.

The business man may sometimes forget an important item even when he has taken pains to enter it in his diary and to keep that diary open before him.

We will give you an instance founded on fact.

Below is a page showing the appointments of a Mr. Williamson for the day:

Monday, July 8th, 2012

Sales Manager, 10 a. m.
Johnson's case
Paper supply
Lunch, Simpson's, with Blake, 1 p. m.
Interview, 2.30 p.m., Jones
Interview, 3.30, Willington, Hendon

You will see there is an appointment for 2.30 p.m. and another some distance away at 3.30. The one at 3.30 was the most important one of the day, but when Mr. Jones came at 2.30 and brought information of a serious import, Mr. Williamson became so absorbed in the possibilities of money-making that he forgot all about the 3.30 appointment until 3.55 p.m.

Mr. Jones was not particularly pleased at the sudden termination of the interview and Mr. Williamson was fifty minutes late in arriving at his destination.

Those minutes cost him exactly $ 250 apiece, for a contract he had hoped to obtain fell through, as he was not present in time to see that his claim was properly presented.

This kind of forgetfulness frequently occurs with men who have good memories, as well as with men who have not good memories.

The bad memory forgets entirely and the good memory forgets because something unusual happens and for the moment crowds out of mind the thing that was to be remembered.

The point to be noted is that if we are to remember a thing *at the right time*, we have need of more than a good memory; we need a systematic handling of our attention.

Thus, if Mr. Williamson had kept a watch on himself, he would not have allowed the interview with Mr. Jones to absorb his interest to the full.

He would have had an eye on the clock without allowing Mr. Jones to know it.

5.2   Degrees of Memory

There is no man who has no memory at all.

There are thousands who have poor memories, a greater number who have fair memories, but the good and the excellent are not so plentiful.

An employee for instance may have a poor memory for general things, a slightly better memory for all the ledger accounts which he handles every day and as we pointed out previously, an excellent memory for the personalities and records of football or cricket.

In this Series of Books we are speaking to men and women who have not succeeded as yet in remembering
things they want to remember.

There is much in life that is too trivial for a permanent
record. For instance, a man says:

"If you ask me what I had for luncheon ten days ago I can
only say I have completely forgotten, because the matter
in itself was unimportant. I have luncheon every day of
my life and I have no food faddisms to trouble me; consequently mental impressions about luncheons are weak.

But if you ask me when I first tasted venison?

I can tell you all about it, although it happened nearly
twenty years ago. I can tell you the people who were at
the table and what we all said. The reason why I remember this incident is its unique variation from the ordinary
meal to which I was accustomed. I forget the ordinary
meal because it is so ordinary and I remember still now
the unique meal because it was unique".

5.3   Selection: Conscious and Unconscious

We have heard it said by an Australian bushman that at
the end of a day's journeying he could recall in minutest
detail all that he had seen between the rising and the
setting of the sun.

No doubt, his powers of observation, trained by necessity, had reached a very high point of efficiency.

But a strict analysis would reveal that the great multitude of objects which he could plainly recall were themselves but a very small proportion of those that had actually met his eye.

Governed by the definite purpose of finding his way to his destination and perhaps at surveying the country so as to be able to retrace his steps, he had, all through the hours of his traveling, been selecting, from among the multitude of impressions that were all streaming in upon him through the sense of sight, those that were relevant to his purpose.

What do we see?

- *"we see, in the fullest sense of the word: only those things that have some definite meaning for us"*.

To the geologist, to the botanist, to the poet, to the historian, to the commercial traveler, to the hunter, to the farmer, one and the same landscape presents many different meanings and so many different aspects of it will be recorded. Our mind is not like a sensitized plate or in a cinematographic film.

Our mind discriminates even in the act of observing.

Its operations are governed always by some purpose more or less explicit.

Even though no definite purpose be presented in consciousness, it is ever choosing the material that is akin to its predominant interest and those masses of organized knowledge that are already most richly furnished are the most avid of new material.

In accordance with this principle at the end of a walk undertaken without any special purpose of observation, it will be found that, of objects that have come into view, certain have set a definite mark.

This is *unconscious* selection.

Even if we set out, on the other hand, with a definite intention of observing all we can of whatever kind, we shall still discover, when we just come to review our own pilgrimage, that:

-   *"those impressions are strongest that have most intimately associated themselves with our previous experience", and*
-   *"with matters in which we are ourselves habitually interested".*

Our mind is looking for some links i.e. associations by himself and is also focused at our habits of interest.

CHAPTER 6: "What to Do – What to Avoid"

6.1   "What to Do"
6.2   The 7 to Do's in a scheme
6.3   "What to Avoid"
6.4   The 7 to Avoid's in a scheme

6.1 "What to Do"

1) Accustom your mind to the fact that the working methods of the BMS-method are based on long years of experience and research.

2) You may not always see how we are going to help you, but proceed confidently and the whole plan will become plain.

3) There is a loss and a gain in every step forward. Something must always be left behind. The loss is not important if you secure the gain: so know clearly what you want, then begin the task, cheerily.

4) Draw up your scale of values. Among the things of most worth are health of body and mind, friends, books, adequate money, inward peace, service to others.

5) To obtain these values you must *work*; they seldom come just of their own accord. Self-expression is the chief method of attraction; it may just as easily attract the confidence of the man of the world as that of the philosopher.

6) Be sure that in the mental world all things may be brought to work together for good. Hence psycho-synthesis. Aim at harmony of all functions both of body and of mind.

7) Believe in your star and in your success. Success will come if you proceed and if you keep your focus.

6.2   The 7 to Do's in a scheme

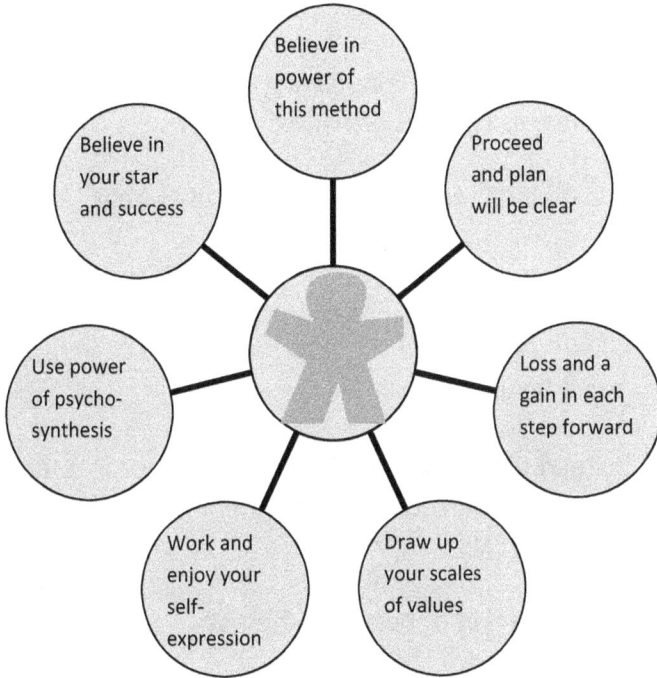

Explanation:

As we can see above, we have 7 to Do's in part II of this book. It all starts with your quiet believe in the power of this method and the power of proceeding and soon the surprising results will come and will be clear for you.

6.3   "What to Avoid"

1)   Avoid being a grumbler

The man with an everlasting grievance usually just grieves his chances out of existence.

2)   Avoid aiming too high, but aim high enough

Adjust your ambition to your abilities and your ambition will grow accordingly.

3)   Avoid bewailing your lot

Instead of thus wasting your energy, use it to find a better position, or in some other ways to enlarge your interests.

4)   Avoid the fear of being laughed at

5)   Avoid the notion that the counsel of the four preceding paragraphs has no real connection with the development of mental efficiency

It has a close connection.

6)   Avoid being satisfied with a low ideal

7)   Avoid the mental attitude of pessimism & fatalism

6.4   The 7 to Avoid's in a scheme

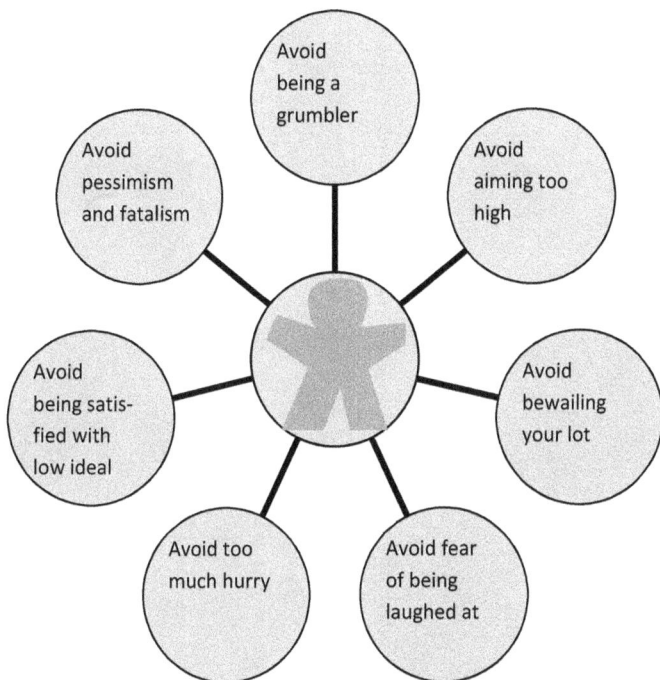

Avoid being a grumbler

Avoid pessimism and fatalism

Avoid aiming too high

Avoid being satisfied with low ideal

Avoid bewailing your lot

Avoid too much hurry

Avoid fear of being laughed at

Explanation:

As we can see above, we have 7 to Avoid's in part II of this book and they are all warning us for a specific mental attitude. Be aware of your thoughts and feelings and just get as successful as you can and which is in your scope.

Chapter 7:   Mental and Health Culture

CHAPTER 7:   Mental and Health Culture Exercises

Also this part of this book will end with some mental and physical exercises just to make sure you will get in the best shape possible in the shortest period of time.

7.1   Mental Exercise 1   Noticing by Taking a Walk

When next you take just a walk abroad, either in *town* or *country*, resolve to notice as much as you can of all the things that are in any degree unusual.

You will, of course, see much that is familiar to you, the same kind of people wearing the same kind of clothes and hear them using the same kind of talk, but keep your eyes and ears open for anything that is out of the common.

Deliberately search for sights and sounds with an element of newness to you. When you have returned from your walk, quickly go over in your mind the route you took.

Then begin your memory exercise by starting at the end of your journey and going *"backwards"* mentally over the ground all the way to the beginning.

This method of the return journey is a little difficult for you at first, but:

"it is one of the finest mental exercises ever prescribed".

You are developing your powers of observation, you are also training your concentration, your memory and your reproductive imagination.

If, during the process of reconstructing your journey from the end to the beginning, you observe weak connections, points at which recollection is difficult, study those weaknesses very closely, because they may reveal memory defects which call for attention.

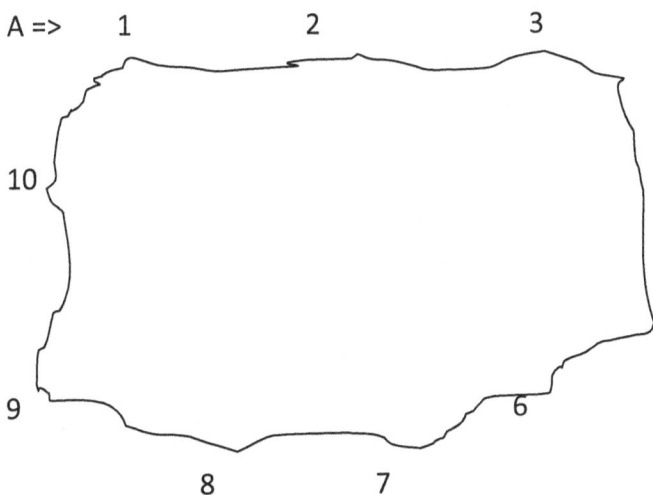

A =>   1   2   3

10

9   6

        8   7

In order to show you how this exercise can be worked out we included a diagram drawn by a student; see above.

A is the starting point. The arrow shows the direction out and home.

The numbers are explained below:

1) Noticed a big Rolls-Royce with No. OA318. Found out afterwards that OA are the registration letters for Birmingham.

2) Clump of Fir trees. They have one side dark green or mossy, the other side quite brown. Why? Is it from the west wind?

3) Church clock stopped at 12 noon. It is Friday and people are agitated. Clock had never stopped for 40 years. Old women quite superstitious and filled with foreboding.

4) Rector's front garden being bedded out in carpet fashion. Effective in a way, but not, perhaps, the best way.

5) In the direction of H, I noticed the three factory chimneys were not *"smoking"*. Inquiry later showed a strike had begun that morning.

6) Motor-cyclist in trouble. Seemed to be biting a piece of copper wire all the time.

7) Policeman at corner on point duty. Never saw one there before.

8) G's poultry farm. Fowls looked too cramped together. What happens when science is overdone?

9) Bullfinch in the hedge. Rather uncommon.

10) Sign at the entrance of a nice cottage garden says: *"Jinger Beer"*; simplified spelling.

We need not complete the list.

Obviously students whose walk is confined to the town will have a different variety of sights to record.

You can probably follow this example, but in exercising this kind of journey by yourself, all that is needed is something like this:

"I was able to reconstruct the whole walk mentally, in inverse order, omitting ... facts which I had not noted at the time, as proved by a second walk".

7.2　Mental Exercise 2　Observation of a Room

The use of a pen and pencil in recording observations is an excellent training in both speed and accuracy.

The next time you visit a friend's house, or the room of any building to which you are a stranger, take two glances round the room and when you get home take four sheets of paper and by means of rough designs or squares, indicate what you can remember of the pictures on the walls.

On a fifth sheet, put down the position of the furniture of the room and indicate the number of tables, chairs and other articles.

Be aware of the fact that your observation power to start with probably is not as strong as you wished and just be assured that your power will grow and grow by training.

7.3   Mental Exercise 3   Hearing of a List of Words

The aim of this exercise is two-fold:

1) first, to discover the span of your own immediate ear memory
2) next, to train that ear memory until its efficiency is greatly increased

Ask a friend to read aloud to you a list of words like the following. It is upon the sound of the words that we wish you to concentrate your attention.

Read one line at a time:

1)   Tree, Fig, Card, Ice
2)   Emboss, Embalm, Day, Joy
3)   Care, Carry, Fustian, Ring
4)   Don't, Subaltern, Gibraltar, Fix
5)   Marry, Cost-accounts, Relay, Women

Keep an account of the number of your mistakes.

Later, practice with longer lines of words.

Like the list which just follows. These are naturally more difficult than the shorter ones and if there are more *"slips"* in recalling them, it should be remembered that: "practice in ear memory will develop more power".

Ear memory work is excellent training for conversation in foreign languages.

Indeed it is a great advantage in every trade or profession to develop to the utmost this valuable memory-factor. It will help you a lot in business as in private life as well:

1)   Tub, Mill, Mix, Cigar, Paper
2)   Scrap, Room, Cork, Fat, Job, Duke
3)   Tube, Joss, Home, China, Fix, Star, Ham
4)   Skill, Teaser, Fob, Jay, Tobacco, Simply, Toil, Jam

The way in which you should note your results is as follows:

"in the first list I had . . . right and . . . wrong".
"in the second list I had . . . right and . . . wrong".

"Wrong" means either an incorrect word, a word in the wrong place, or inability to recall a word.

Note. You should really endeavor to practice every day the exercises belonging to the book in hand.

In addition, we advise you to practice the earlier exercises in rotation, one or two daily, as you are able to. In Part II of this book we give you 3 mental exercises and also 4 physical. The first to improve your mental efficiency of course and the second to improve your health culture.

All the Exercises described in the first part of this book may be briefly reviewed each morning.

Suggestions for this purpose will be found at the end of each part of this book.

Individual variations will often make the work much more pleasant. Original combinations may be tried: if the new attempts include the old ideas, the result should be the same.

7.4   Physical Exercise 1   Elevator no 2

As soon as you are out of bed and remember not to jump out, but to crawl out, STAND STRAIGHT and just breathe deeply, using the arms as in the exercises described in Part I of this book. Raise them forward over the head while breathing in and lower them sideways while exhaling. The chest walls would be lifted upward now and the lower ribs forced outward.

7.5   Physical Exercise 2   Stretching no 1

A very simple stretching exercise is the following: stand close to the wall and facing it, say about a foot from it. Then, with an ordinary pin in the right hand, reach up and stick the pin into the wall as high as you can reach. Rise on the toes to increase the height. The next movement is to reach up with the left hand and remove the pin.

While in this position try to raise the pin an inch higher with the left hand. Now repeat the operation with the right hand, but do not touch the wall with the hands or with any part of the body. A small pin and light pressure will not injure the finest wall-paper or paint.

Repeat the STAND STRAIGHT exercise number 1 of part I of this book, standing against the edge of the door, heels, hips, back of chest and head against the door edge.

Now raise the arms sideways and upwards and if the height of the door permits, try to clasp the fingers over the top of the door. Gently pull the body upwards without raising the heels from the floor.

Hold this position for five seconds, then lower the arms and relax. Repeat this four or five times.

If you cannot reach the top of the door, try to stretch your hands upwards as high as possible without altering your original position. You will find that you have on your sides muscles that you never before knew were there.

7.6   Physical Exercise 3   Warming up

Take the WARMING UP exercise of Part I of this book and make the arm work more rapid and the slapping of the back more vigorous. This increases stimulation without any undue exertion.

7.7   Physical Exercise 4   Golf Drive

Stand in front of your mirror with the feet about 16 or 18 inches apart and the hands clasped in front of the body at about the level of the waist.

Grasp the left thumb with the right hand. You are supposed to be attempting a golf drive. Raise the arms over the right shoulder. Imagine that you have a golf club in your hands. Turn the body to the right, leaving the right foot in place and pivoting on the toes of the left foot. Keep your eyes on a spot half-way between your feet, as if you were watching the ball. Be sure to emphasize the body twist so that you are actually looking down at the floor over the left shoulder. Then swing the arms sideways and downwards and across the body, as if hitting the ball. The arms are carried upward to the left and over the left shoulder. As the arms cross the body the weight is carried on to the left foot and the body is turned to the left.

There will be just enough body twist to make it necessary to raise the right heel from the floor.

This is called the "FOLLOW THROUGH".

Bring the arms, with the fingers still interlocked, well up on the left, at least as high as the head. This is a fairly accurate copy of the real action in a golf drive and we will speak of it hereafter as the "GOLF DRIVE".

While no movement on the golf links calls for a similar movement on the left side, we must remember that we are trying to exercise the entire body by rather popular methods.

Therefore, to accomplish this result, the exercise should be repeated, using the drive from left to right.

The mental image, the correct *"stance"*, or the correct position, a steady, forceful swing and a high *"follow through"* will make this an especially helpful exercise.

7.8   Suggestions for the day

Is exactly the same suggestion as in Part I of this book:

-       *"get some out-of-door exercise each day
        and try a brisk walk of about 1000 meters".*

Hold the head high, the chest well up, swing your arms well across the body and breathe very deeply every few minutes. Think of your Hopi dance as you step along.

Don't take your business troubles with you; take a congenial companion. Just enjoy your walk and have some fun.

Suggestions for some review: Stand Straight, Warming Up, Breathing and the great and humoristic Hopi Dance and just have some fun by doing these exercises. Enjoy!

7.9   The 7 Exercises of Part 2 in a scheme

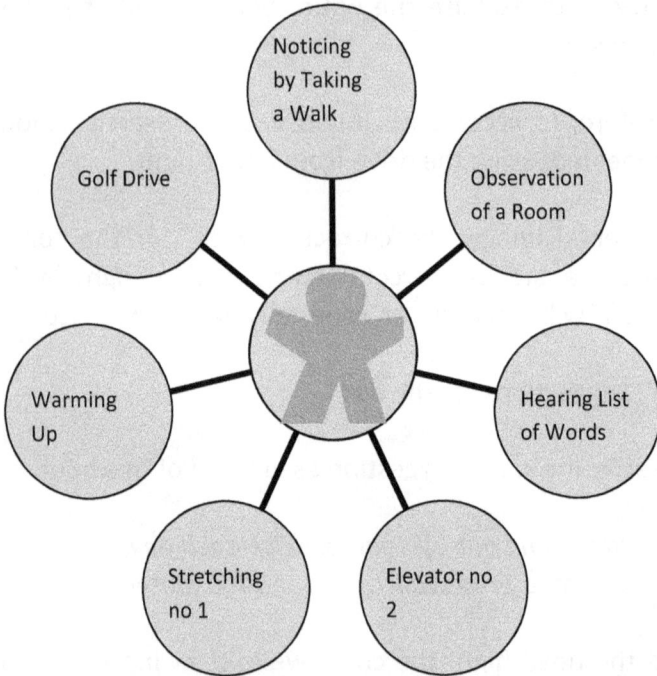

Explanation:

We have put the exercises of this part in a scheme again from a didactic perspective point of view. You will see that this scheme will help you to remember the exercises almost automatically & easily and that's just our purpose.

7.10   Book 2 in this series of books

What is coming next?

You have heard people say: *"there are so many things I want to do and ought to do, but I never seem able to make a start"*. Other people complain that they have no difficulty in making a start, but they never finish.

Others, again, allow their plans to suffer because of their feelings*: "I'm not in the mood for duty"*, they say.

All of these aspects of weakness in Will-Power and many others, are dealt with in book no 2:

-       *"how to improve your Will-Power?"*

7.11   Afterword

We are now at the end of the first book of this series of 7 books. I hope you enjoyed as much reading as I enjoyed writing this book for you. After all this series of books will help you to achieve in Life what you want and perhaps even more important these books will help you also to find out what your heart is after. Isn't that the big deal?

For myself do I have to thank my little daughter Yara. Yara you are the greatest inspiration of my life and also a great example for me. Your father sends you all his purest love.